PROTECT

ONLINE

IDENTITY

LIKE YOUR

VIRGINITY

ABHISHEK SINGH RAJPUROHIT

INDIA · SINGAPORE · MALAYSIA

Notion Press

Old No. 38, New No. 6
McNichols Road, Chetpet
Chennai - 600 031

First Published by Notion Press 2018
Copyright © Abhishek Singh Rajpurohit 2018
All Rights Reserved.

ISBN 978-1-68466-293-7

Index

Acknowledgments

I am no Shakespeare, but after working in marketing and digital advertising for some time now, I've been asked by lots of my clients and students alike about the idea of writing a book.

There are hundreds of books that tinker with the topics like what to do online, how to market your brand or yourself. But when I started researching about how many books were written to educate on what not to do online, I found very few on this topic, and thus the gestation of this book took place.

I am really thankful to my wife, Gayatri, who steadfastly supported my career in digital marketing and encouraged my writing. She gave me valuable advice at many critical junctures, and without her, this book would have been impossible. My business partner, Abhishek Mittal was enthusiastic about the book, and he, while running the business, rearranged parts of his schedules and took a lot of workload off my shoulders so that I could carve out extra placid moments to finish the manuscript.

My parents, Narpat Singh Rajpurohit and Archana Singh Rajpurohit, and my brother, Navodaya Singh Rajpurohit, helped me navigate the contracts, (and the latter also helped me format the book). They also helped collate my thoughts and offered me advice and perspective from the outset of the project.

Last but not least, I'm blessed that many people throughout my life, from teachers and professors to friends and colleagues, have encouraged me and told me that I'm a good writer.

To all of you, I'm very thankful.

Introduction

This book is not about hacking. Instead, it dabbles in the increasing peril of the digital world around us. It is my humble attempt to shed some light on how technology is invading every aspect of our daily lives, how we as a species are reacting to it, and how we can secure ourselves and our future generations from this ever-growing devil.

The book is meant for people who are active online and are looking for new ways to find out how they can increase their defense against troll, hackers and other people who are always looking to get a pie from their financial and personal portfolio.

Online reputation risks are often multiplied for businesses, and thus, companies need to look far beyond how search results impact one person's name. These organizations need to protect their names, brands and their products from many online threats. Negative reviews can hurt sales, social media missteps can open up costly litigation, and reputational risks can even hide beneath the surface of the web.

To fan the flame, online and offline reputation have started merging. Today, traditional word-of-mouth advertising is amplified by online channels, and customer service often begins with an online interaction through a public social media channel.

Whether companies like it or not, consumers have learned that reaching out to companies on sites like Twitter often elicits a response more quickly than calling a customer service line. If an EMS (Enterprise Messaging System) connection to a company is known on social media, then it highly possible that a customer may contact them. Also, in some instances, customers specifically try to go around customer service departments to get questions answered—or if they are frustrated.

Many consumers, and millennials, in particular, expect that a company will respond on social media channels. It is bolstered by the fact that many major corporations are effectively using Twitter as a customer service channel. Companies like Nike and UPS actively engage customers on Twitter and promote this use of its platform and to offer specific tools for businesses. For instance, a company can now quickly add a link to tweets that automatically display a call to action button, by which the customer can send the business a direct Twitter message. Some companies are receiving a growing number of customer user requests through social media, and they are embracing it because in some cases, it is significantly cheaper than staffing a call center. In fact, many businesses now include their Twitter handles on their customer service pages, giving customers an option to call, e-mail or reach out on Twitter.

For individuals, both young and old, this book acknowledges that we all make mistakes, and we will continue to make them. It will teach you to understand online vulnerability to build a reputational firewall and protect your identity like your virginity. This book discusses the different types of online nightmares, ways to handle them and, hopefully, to prevent them. Some of it is common sense (the best defense to your reputation is keeping your nose clean), and other aspects are counterintuitive (you don't stay off the grid). It will teach you how the proliferation of digital cameras in mobile phones, surveillance devices, drones and standard-issue police equipment makes us vulnerable.

Lastly, this book explains the many ways that companies and individuals can build their online reputation.

Marketing in a Nutshell

You see a gorgeous girl at a party. You go up to her and say, "I am very rich. Marry me!" That's direct marketing.

You're at a party with a bunch of friends and see a gorgeous girl. One of your friends goes up to her and pointing at you says, "He's very rich. Marry him." That's advertising.

You see a gorgeous girl at a party. You go up to her and get her telephone number. The next day, you call and say, "Hi, I'm very rich. Marry me." That's telemarketing.

You're at a party and see a gorgeous girl. You get up and straighten your tie, you walk up to her and pour her a drink, you open the door (of the car) for her, pick up her bag after she drops it, offer her a ride and then say, "By the way, I'm rich. Will you marry me?" That's public relations.

You're at a party and see a gorgeous girl. She walks up to you and says, "You are very rich! Can you marry me?" That's brand recognition.

You see a gorgeous girl at a party. You go up to her and say, "I am very rich. Marry me!" She gives you a nice hard slap on your face. That's customer feedback.

You see a gorgeous girl at a party. You go up to her and say, "I am very rich. Marry me!" And she introduces you to her husband. That's the demand and supply gap.

You see a gorgeous girl at a party. You go up to her, and before you say anything, another person comes and tells her, "I'm rich. Will you marry me?" and she goes with him. That's competition eating into your market.

You see a gorgeous girl at a party. You go up to her and before you say, "I'm rich. Marry me!" Your wife arrives. That's restriction from entering new markets.

Digital Ninjas

A ninja was a covert agent or mercenary in feudal Japan. The functions of ninjas included espionage, sabotage, infiltration, assassination and guerrilla warfare. Their methods of waging irregular warfare were deemed dishonorable and beneath the samurai who observed strict rules about honor and combat.

A ninja can be defined as a person who excels in a particular skill, and these digital ninjas are highly skilled in capturing your online lives.

Digital slaughter begins as a willful act by someone who wishes to harm you or your brand intentionally and uses anonymity as a tool while attacking you. His words convert into swords to be shoved into the gut.

Digital slaughtering is most effective when others like conspirators or unknowing parrots are incited by social media. The result is multiple slices and stabs, leaving permanent, searchable Internet records that continue to harm your brand, fan base, business, reputation among friends, customers, visitors, or other media on a 24/7 basis.

When a negative thread appears about you on the Internet, you never know the intensity of the attack and where all it has been hit. And the most astonishing fact about a digital slaughtering is that the wounds will open even after a few years when someone searches for you or your brand's name.

We will talk about multiple instances of this kind of attack throughout this book. Then, what can be done to counter this will be discussed.

To be sure, new technology is transformative. Moreover, it is overwhelmingly good, improving the way we live, work, shop, educate and love. It changes societies with unprecedented transparency. It, however, also has a dark side. We will explore how this dark side can threaten your reputation, brand and business through online attacks.

Too much of commentary about the misuse of Internet platforms is lost in the power and breadth of this technology. The Internet, no less than the Industrial Revolution, is reshaping every aspect of our life. Facebook is the world's third largest country (If a number of users are equated to the population of a country). Generated content is forcing businesses to be responsive to the customer unlike before. Adaptive information technology may be our best bet at educating the planet.

Digital technology has swept the world like a huge positive force. However, we overlook the fact that because digital technology is woven into almost everything we do and think, this technology also has a raging dark side which includes digital slaughtering.

In a digital world, we need to approach technology with higher skill. The youth needs to approach and use tech with greater wisdom.

While black hats (hackers) can't match the prowess of foreign governments in accessing government computers, they have more than enough skill to sneak into a digital device you own. So, if you are wondering if your digital devices are compromised in some way, you can stop worrying for the fire has already reached the village.

The ease with which digital slayers and potential blackmailers access your machines for damaging information to use against you is not just limited to the messages you've ever sent, any website you have ever visited, or any secret-individual or financial details, account numbers and PIN numbers that you not want anyone to know about, in any of your computers, but extends way beyond them. What this means is that even if you are warily watching your back, you are still susceptible to these perpetrators.

Like these susceptible American users of Facebook who were shocked to find that their private data was compromised by their dear social media site to tamper the 2016 presidential elections. This is also known as Cambridge Analytica.

Camera phones capture fascinating pictures every day. In its advertising, Apple brags about the quality of its iPhone cameras, and GoPro cameras document the most harrowing situations in high-definition brilliance.

Cameras capture the good and the bad, the cop and the robber, the perpetrator and the victim. Because of this proliferation, people get photographed and filmed doing bad things.

I still remember the time I was interning with a hotel in Mumbai and one of my friends came and broke the news of a new MMS. This was in the year 2005 and accessing a smartphone was a challenging task. However, curiosity always wins, and we figured out who all in our hostel had a smartphone and eventually located one of them (There were many. Around 180 boys) in the hostel and ended up knocking his door at one in the morning (not that he was sleeping).

The MMS I am talking about was one of the first Bollywood scandals in which a failing Gujarati actor, whose sister was one of the top actresses at that time, was shown in a compromising position with a famous Bengali actress.

That video was one of the first clip to go viral, and it clearly showed us the power of this devil in the coming years.

"Everywhere you go, everyone has a camera," said comedian Robin Williams. "It's not Big Brother anymore, it's Little Snitch," he had said. The Internet is the new camera of the twenty-first century. It is always on. Snitch hides in video cameras, cell phone cameras and tiny pinhole cameras disguised in pens or on lapels or in reading or sunglasses.

In 2009 came the mother of all pranks, when two young Dominos Pizza's employees in rural North Carolina filmed themselves sneezing and blowing their noses on Dominos food and indulging in another bizarre behavior (that cannot be mentioned here).

In no time, 750,000 people had viewed the video, and Dominos was reeling and struggling to get the word out that the two employees had not served the disgusting pizza to customers.

https://www.youtube.com/watch?v=OhBmWx QpedI&t=29s

About forty-eight hours later, Dominos president Patrick posted a sincere YouTube response in which he thanked the online community for allowing him to take immediate action issuing arrest warrants to the employees and sanitizing the store. He ended his two-minute apology with an impassioned talk about the damage the company's owners and 125,000 employees had suffered due to the incident.

This was a bold move, a light-speed reaction according to the standards of traditional media relations. In this new global, digital world, the authors advise clients to view eight hours as one digital day. By this standard, Doyle was late by five digital days. "The lag in response time left the online conversation to grow and fester, and the story continued to proliferate throughout social media channels," wrote Patrick Vogt of Forbes.

The truly effective response would have been mounted within hours. Sales still sagged, and within months, Dominos unveiled a new humility campaign, launching a total repositioning of its product.

Recently in 2018, Dominos India was targeted by a so-called BBC documentary in which an ex-chef working at Dominos was shown talking about how your cheese burst pizza is not cheese but a concoction of mayonnaise and is not suitable for health.

https://www.youtube.com/watch?v=8NErLp9jlJI

The video was shot in a typical documentary style, and with clever editing, the Director General of Dominos was also shown in the video where he was asked by a journalist about the 'fake cheese' and gave a sullen response.

The video became instantly famous, and I received the same video on WhatsApp from at least three people. And my mother prohibited me from eating pizzas from Dominos, Pizza Hut and also the ones made by my wife.

Later, a counterattack video was shot and popularized by Dominos which was an official response showing that the aforementioned video was not right. However, the sales of Dominos slumped as the damage was already done in the minds of innocent consumers for the rest of their lives.

(http://www.forbesindia.com/article/special/dominos-fake-cheese-video-turns-out-to-be-fake/49975/1)

That kind of viral shame would have been impossible without the Internet. For today's new kind of celebrity, a scandal is the only reason for fame—that can have a significant potential to inflict collateral damage on everyone they know. A few people, who are publicly embarrassed like Paris Hilton or Kim Kardashian, find their shame to be a golden road to riches. However, that doesn't stop thousands of users from trying.

Puke University's 2010 graduate Karen Owen, created 'Fuck List,' a PowerPoint thesis of the men she had slept with, rating their attributes complete with a professional-looking case study approach, including bar charts. The fact that she may have believed it would be shared with just a few friends did not stop it from becoming a global sensation that brought her a flood of queries from agents, publishers and movie producers.

We Indians are known for making celebrities out of ordinary citizens, and the history is full of people like Dhinchak Pooja and Dancing Uncle, and we love these controversial semi-celebrities on our prime time shows like Bigg Boss, MTV roadies, etc.

https://www.bbc.com/news/world-asia-india-44353069

https://timesofindia.indiatimes.com/tv/news/hindi/dhinchak-pooja-to-return-to-tv-after-bigg-boss-11-with-this-show/articleshow/61657972.cms

These were just a few examples that show how much the line between offline and online has blurred and how will these two worlds merge into one in the near future.

"Your brand isn't what you say it is; it's what Google says it is."

— Chris Anderson

Online Reputation Management

More than half of the web users are somewhat knowledgeable about social media. Some are adept at using it for product publicity and promotion. Yet most people still do not have solid plans and strategies to counter digital attacks.

The Internet is now a central feature of risk management for brands and products. Most Multinational companies have yet to become sensitive to what is being said about them which lends them into the same boat with other small, online businesses like restaurants, doctors and local businesses.

In short, businesses or individuals, celebrities or nonprofits choose to scroll unprotected through this new war zone. Many senses but not truly understand how the law treats digital media differently from offline media.

In the movie *The Dark Knight*, Batman (Bruce Wayne) has trouble deciphering the motives of his nemesis, the Joker. Michael Caine's character, butler Alfred Pennyworth, speaks of his experience tracking a bandit.

Bruce Wayne: (Watching the tape the Joker broadcast on the news) Killing me won't get their money back. I knew the mob wouldn't go down without a fight, but this is different they have crossed the line.

Alfred: You crossed the line first, sir. You squeezed and hammered them to the point of desperation. So, in their desperation, they turned to a man they didn't fully understand.

Bruce Wayne: Criminals aren't complicated, Alfred. We need to figure out what he's after.

Alfred: With all due respect, Master Wayne, perhaps this is a man that you don't fully understand. When I was in Burma, a long time ago, my friends and I were working for the local government. They were trying to buy the loyalty of tribal leaders by bribing them with precious stones. However, their caravans were being raided in a forest north of Rangoon by a bandit. So, we started looking for the rocks. However, after six months, we couldn't find anyone who had traded with him.

One day I saw a child playing with a ruby the size of a tangerine. The bandit had been throwing the stones away.

Bruce Wayne: Then why steal them?

Alfred: Because he thought it was a good sport. Because some men aren't looking for anything logical, like money. They can't be bought, bullied, reasoned or negotiated with. Some men want to watch the world burn.

Brandjacking

'Brandjacking' is an activity whereby someone acquires or otherwise assumes the online identity of another entity to acquire that person's or business's brand equity.

Brandjacking is as old as a phenomenon as our old Indian scriptures, whether it was when Sri Krishna disguised as Mohini to kill Bhasmasur or when Human masqueraded as an old monkey to trick Bheem.

https://en.wikipedia.org/wiki/Bhasmasura_(Hinduism)

But brandjacking for a brand or an individual is no more acceptable. A brand could be destroyed because of a brandjacking, and there have been multiple cases when a brand or an individual had to pay a hefty price for being a bit negligent.

Name Jackers

'Cybersquatting' or 'Domain squatting' is a derogatory term for registering terms as Internet domain names that do not belong to the registrant. Personal name registration is also known as 'namejacking.'

The most prominent case of name hijacking has happened with one of the most beloved and influential companies in the world aka Google.

When Google decided to become a part of a bigger brand and to name that brand 'alphabet,' they were baffled to find that the name alphabet was not available and a car brand owned it. The car brand refused to let go of the website name. The irony of this situation was that the company that usually decides the fate of other websites was bested by one. This goes to show how unforgiving the web can be, and if a giant like Google is helpless against namejacking, you can already imagine what can it do to mere mortals like us.

(https://techcrunch.com/2015/08/10/google-is-now-alphabet-but-it-doesnt-own-alphabet-com/)

On 9th August 2013, Indian travelers were perplexed to see when they tried to open a famous booking portal online, they were getting redirected to a domain parking server. The website was down for approximately 12 hours, and according to sources, they lost approximately Rs. 2–3 crore of revenue just in that period.

https://www.gadgetsnow.com/tech-news/Yatra-com-site-down-as-company-forgets-to-renew-domain-name/articleshow/21768718.cms

The Streisand Effect

The Streisand Effect, as explained by Wikipedia, is a phenomenon whereby an attempt to hide, remove or censor a piece of information has the unintended consequence of publicizing the information more widely, usually facilitated by the Internet. In a nutshell, it means *don't make matters worse by chatting online about or causing others to link to the offending site(s), which will only raise its prominence.*

In July 2011, a request was made by the British Phonographic Industry asking The Pirate Bay to remove torrent links of the copyrighted music of the company's members. The torrent site refused, which forced the company to go to court. In April 2012, the High Court of the United Kingdom ordered five major Internet service providers to block access to the torrent's site. This proved to be a terrible move that only increased The Pirate Bay's popularity. The block was set up on May 1, 2012, but around 12 million visitors, more than the site has ever received, accessed The Pirate Bay that day. Right after the block was set up, the torrent site gave users easy ways to get around it, allowing the uninterrupted access of torrent links that The Pirate Bay hosted.

Online Shaming is a form of Internet vigilantism in which targets are publicly humiliated using technology like social and new media. Proponents of shaming see it as a form of online participation that allows hacktivists and cyber-dissidents to justify injustices. Critics see it as a tool that encourages online mobs to destroy the reputation and careers of people or organizations that made perceived slights.

Online shaming frequently involves the publication of private information on the Internet (called doxing), which can frequently lead to hate messages and death threats being used to intimidate that person. The ethics of public humiliation have been a source of debate over privacy and ethics.

Revenge Porn or **Revenge Pornography** is the distribution of sexually explicit images or video of individuals without their consent. The sexually explicit images or video may be made by a partner of an intimate relationship with the knowledge and consent of the subject, or it may be made without his or her knowledge. The possession of the material may be used by the perpetrators to blackmail the subjects into performing other sex acts, to coerce them into continuing the relationship or to punish them for ending one.

Google Bowling

Most businesses engage in Search Engine Optimization (SEO), a technique to raise the rankings of one's own website. Google bowling works just the opposite way. When Google determines that a business or brand has been using automated spam to raise its profile artificially, it ruthlessly kicks the website down in the rankings, often with no appeal and little explanation.

Google bowling occurs when attackers go about manipulating anchor text (or other SEO strategies like link building) in a way that appears to be benefiting you or your company. As a result, Google will punish your website, burying your company or product at the bottom of the search results.

"You are who Google says you are," writes Anna Vander Broek in her article, 'Managing Your Online Identity,' on *Forbes.*

Customer Service

Businesses today have to offer customer service as never before because individuals today have the power to punish, the likes of which were never seen before.

KIT KAT CASE STUDY

A viral video appeared to be a Kit Kat commercial in which an office worker in a soulless office takes a break by unwrapping the candy bar and taking a bite. Instead of a satisfying moment and the favorite company jingle, however, blood starts to squirt from the man's mouth. He doesn't see that he has in fact bitten into the dismembered finger of an orangutan. The point of the video post, produced by Green peace, was to protest Nestle's use of palm oil in Indonesia, which leads the deforestation of the orangutan's native habitat.

Nestle, which had already committed to shifting to environmental certified palm oil, asked YouTube to remove the video. This, of course, activated the Streisand Effect to ensure it would go viral.

Anybody can now draw on the power of social media to task the crowd to assemble secrets to ruin a target or force a change in policies. These are also social engineering techniques that involve hacking people, spooling them into divulging secrets, often to gain access to their computer networks. In this way, they trick the companies that run web-based systems into giving hackers the keys to their private digital kingdoms.

"Being a nationalistic hacker is pretty much the coolest thing you can do as a child in China," Tom Kellermann, who has served on the US Commission on Cybersecurity, is quoted as saying in the book *Digital Assassination:* **Protecting** *Your Reputation, Brand, or Business Against Online Attacks* by Richard Torrenzano, Mark Davis. *"They have competitions within their provinces for the best hacker, and the winner gets taken care of for life. They are given somewhere to live, a regular salary, and then they work for a shell company that allows them to do whatever they want, provided that when they find anything interesting, they share it with the government,"* he continues.

"We see hacking as evil, and we treat good hackers as evil," Kellermann continues. *"They nurture them. The Chinese government has the only one rule—and that rule is 'Don't hack us.' And if you do find something interesting, like a US-owned system, or you can infiltrate something within the United States, let us know. There is a sense of nationalism around the tradecraft that is cyberespionage. The use of non-stare actor proxies by regimes like China and Russia is over,"* he says.

Trolling

Tricks are meant to elicit Lulz (a typographical subversion of the word LOL). But, Lulz is something more. It's savoring other people's consternation, grief, horror, disgust, anger and bewilderment.

When campaigns are launched against a brand, business or individual, digital attackers often attack through a front organization. The cutout or front can be non-governmental organizations (NGOs), a reasonable-sounding blog on the Internet, or a vendetta website masquerading as a high-minded news source.

In a social media world, there is often no need to pay people to feign interest in phony campaigns when many issues have a built-in following that can be inspired through social networks. When prominent organizations find their interests under challenge, they often use a digital thread to locate and activate people who are already in passionate agreement them.

TRUTH REMIX

The Internet's retention of any facts especially negative ones enables the remixing of the truth, a slander that has some basis in reality. The loss of context occurs when a contrary fact is indiscriminately mixed in with the divine. It is called truth remix, a tactic that happens in online reviews, in sexual harassment accusations, and the premature release of information about technology products.

Truth remix is helped by the arbitrary and often inaccurate nature of search engine results pages, biased aggregator websites and our own viral rants. Efforts at social-forgetting and name-changing will always get defeated by technology and the human will to remember the worst about people. The result can be a falsehood polluting politics, distorting history and perhaps inciting, provocative philippics that instigate real violence.

There have been multiple instances of movie piracy in India and internationally, but *Udta Punjab* which was released in 2016 takes the cake. It led to a huge financial loss for the producers of the movie.

https://blastatrumpet.wordpress.com/2016/06/18/udta-punjab/udta-punjab-poster/

CORPORATE ESPIONAGE

When an Apple engineer left the prototype of the next generation iPhone by a bar stool in the Gourmet Haus Staudt in Redwood City, California, a patron took it home, realized what it was, and sold it to Gizmodo for $5,000. The result was the reporting, months in advance, of the characteristics of a prototype that was far from being ready for public release. The mistake also blew Apple's chance to reap the benefit of shaping the release of its information and worth millions of marketing dollars.

More deliberate leaks, those not involving beer, happen all the time to technology companies. When it is time to unveil a new consumer technology product, companies strive for the big reveal. With a vast colony of tech bloggers vying for a scoop and no lack of insiders willing to leak details, the big reveal is more often the long and inaccurate tease.

Another case study that you can learn from is of the trouble Research In Motion (Parent company of BlackBerry) had in unveiling the new permutations of its BlackBerry. Another site for premature releases months in advance through unofficial sources was Engadget, which sparked criticism of the devices' perceived shortcomings in one further detail or another, without the context of the overall plot. Crank bloggers picked apart every new function and stylistic detail.

Radia Tape Case

In 2008, the famous Radia tape case, telephonic conversations between Niira Radia (a public relations veteran) and top corporates (Ratan Tata and Mukesh Ambani), top politicians (A Raja, Dravida Munnetra Kazhagam supremo Karunanidhi's daughter Kanimozhi, who was herself a Member of the Parliament), top journalists (Barkha Dutt, Vir Sanghvi, among many others), Atal Bihari Vajpayee's son-in-law Ranjan Bhattacharya and a host of other movers and shakers, were taped by the income tax department and were leaked which revealed Radia's attempt to crack deals on behalf of the Tatas in relation to the 2G spectrum sale. The tapes revealed how corporate lobbyists were taking out information from the Indian government based on their contacts with the media and top officials. This led to the loss of US $4.9 billion for the Union government.

"If you have something that you don't want anyone to know, maybe you shouldn't be doing it in the first place."

— **Eric Schmidt**

A Brave New World

Some 46 percent of men reported that they would be embarrassed if someone saw their browsing history. And someone may well see it. A study by Stanford and Carnegie Mellon Universities finds that the mode (incognito mode) of the four major browsers is no absolute defense against one's searches exposed from within the house or from without increasing exposure to embarrassment. It is a technological development that has been scaling up for more than a century.

The world has moved on. Media that was once so alarming now seems quaint. In the twenty-first century, facial recognition software is advancing toward a state in which users will be able to snap a cell phone image of someone they pass by on the street, subject the image to a Google search, and receive all photos of that person on the web.

The digital world is also acquiring hardware and extensions to follow us around. Personal drones are coming to the market; there are small hovering

AVs that can carry onboard cameras and thermal imaging technology to track and record every move of yours.

Day by day we move forward, believing that there will be no adverse consequences to our exposure. Day by day, we live in a brave new world.

We accept an implicit bargain when we use web-based platforms (the various sites at our fingertips, an array of powerful services for free) in exchange for the ability to track our wants and desires and report them to advertisers. For most people, this deal is acceptable, even if it does make one a little queasy thanks to the use of pseudonymous identifiers. It allows Google and other big players to attach details about our interests and demographic formation to a particular cookie, without correlating it with information that identifies us as individuals.

We have learned to delete our cookies, so companies now track fingerprints, the unique timestamps and other settings to identify you. So increasingly, advertisers are using colored devices, whether computers or cell phones, giving them reputations based on our searches, the things we buy and matching them with our demographic information.

The apps in our cell phones can also follow us, telling advertisers which stores we visit in real time.

UBER DIVORCE CONTROVERSY

In France, Uber is facing a lawsuit after a man's wife was alerted to his location while he was cheating on her with another woman. The husband had requested a car using his wife's phone. But the app continued to send notifications to her phone about his whereabouts even though he had logged out of the account. The couple is now divorced, but the businessman filed a lawsuit against Uber worth £39 million (45 million Euros).

https://metro.co.uk/2017/07/20/divorce-lawyers-now-using-uer-data-to-catch-out-cheats-in-courts-6793416/

We are dependent as never before on the digital devices that copy, store, enact almost every transaction. An exabyte is a billion, or 1 by 18 zeros. By 2010, humanity required 40.8 exabytes of space for new data, or 2.7 gigabytes for every man and woman, on the planet. And yet we continue to grow dependent on systems with data that is utterly insecure. More than 221 million records containing individuals' personal data were compromised in 608 incidents in 2009.

So how do you safeguard yourself from this upcoming brave world?

1. Defend your personal and small business computers with the latest version of three layers of defense—the best firewall, the best antivirus, and the best antispyware software products.

2. Software like Symantec and McAfee. Microsoft Security Essentials are one of the best free antivirus software. If you are a more sophisticated user and a more likely target, however, you might use quality but lesser known security products, since 'firewall killers' are most frequently built for the most popular programs.

3. Set your software security settings to automatic update.

4. Keep up with automatic updates to keep your software and web browsers current.

5. If you have a wireless connection at home, reset the router password with your passcode, a robust series of numbers, letters, and code (the funky little symbols on your keyboard) and finable wireless encryption so you won't be an open store to your neighbor or anyone passing by on the street.

6. You cannot secure a home wireless network. If this is intolerable, go with a hard wire. However, if you do use a router, guard it with that elaborate passcode to make it more secure.

An excellent way to create a password hack is to think about your favorite actress as a child. For example, if it was Ayesha Takia, create your password which is similar to A@#$%A^&* (but it should definitely not be your phone number or your birthday). This password is not unbreakable, but this is better than your name and 1234.

Once you've created your passcodes, share them only with your spouse, only if you are reasonably confident that you are not headed for a divorce. Configure your webmail account—Yahoo!, Hotmail, Google—to https (the 's' is for secure) instead of HTTP. Shop on https websites, and look for the lock icon in your browser frame. You can consider the Electronic Frontier Foundation's 'HTTPS Everywhere' plug-in. It forces websites wherever possible to use https standard.

"We have to abandon the idea that schooling is something restricted to youth. How can it be, in a world where half the things a man knows at 20 are no longer true at 40—and half the things he knows at 40 had been discovered when he was 20?"

— *Arthur C. Clarke*

"Your brand is what people say about you when you're not in the room."

— Jeff Bezos

Ndovu Wawili Wakisongana, Ziumiazo Ni Nyika (When Elephants Jostle, What Gets Hurt Is the Grass)

How can technology change us? How can it reshape society? How will technology affect our concerns about security and privacy? Above all, what fresh challenges will we be facing within a few years that will be as unexpected as those we are grappling with now?

We should first take a step back and assess the changing technology and media landscape. It is more of a combat space, one in which Facebook and Google struggle for dominance. Cyber insecurity will grow, reputational wars will open up in the new area of combat marketing, and reformers will look more and more to the best practices and commercial world for answers.

Google is our great window on the world. Facebook is the mirror in which humanity sees its rejection. These are two distinct models of the Internet, and like two healthy plants in the same pot, they are slow to strangle each other.

The insight of Google was revolutionary, a little notion that a page is determined by how many inbound links there are to that page. Facebook is working to deliver search results based on a different proxy for popularity on what you and your friends have liked in the past.

In 2018, the window and the mirror were starting to look a little more alike. Google Social Search lets you see what your friends 'like' which is Google's response to Facebook, one that allows for more discrete separation of friends by categories. Facebook lets aggressive promotion like a breach in a walled garden, and some social media watchers are predicting Facebook will open up more of its data to search indexes.

	Google	Facebook
Marketing Focus	Targeted Searches Traffic	Friends of Existing Fans
Free Traffic Approach	SEO: Search Engine Optimization	NEO: Networking Engine Optimization
Paid Traffic Platform	AdWords	Facebook Ads
Free Strategy	Generate Quality Backlinks	Generate Quality Engagement
Paid Strategy	Send to High Conversion Pages	Send to High Conversion Updates

Facebook and Google remain two fundamentally different ways of approaching the world.

Google is the great democratic leveler that incentivizes the breaking of all walls so that everyone and everything can be found. This is a transformative technology, though it might be undone to a degree by the proliferation of apps that bypass traditional search to go straight to transactions.

Facebook, meanwhile, chips away at Google's idea of unlimited threatening to break up the Internet into small islands of social groups. Increasingly, we will be tempted to e-mail, exchange videos, buy-sell, make friends and set up events on Facebook through the graph, or nodes of our friends, their recommendations and shared experiences online without ever venturing out into the full world.

Like compound interest, which transforms pennies into fortunes, the potential growth in computing power continues to create media promise to be millions of times more potent than anything we enjoy. The most apparent shift will be the way in which technology is ever more vivid. The vibrant images on today's HDTV sink into our brain in a way that the ghostly shadows of the black and white of the first Philco, or even the flat, pixilated color of conventional television never did. With 3-D without goggles and telepresence (the use of virtual reality technology, especially for remote control of machinery or for apparent participation in distant events) around the corner, we are fast approaching a time when the term virtual reality will no longer be an exaggeration.

As media experience becomes richer and more tactile, man and the most disruptive technologies will sneak up on us. Take for example, Bell Labs Picturephone that dazzled millions at the 1964 World Fair in New York never took hold.

Then suddenly, when the idea of a videophone seemed like a relic of the world of the future exhibit, Skype subversively infiltrated our laptops. Many new technologies will crop up like Skype, especially as television fully converges with the Internet.

Mobile devices, of course, will be thinner, faster and less expensive, with stronger batteries. Appliances will be smarter networked, and most content will be device agnostic.

AND THUS ENTERS THE THIRD ELEPHANT: AMAZON WITH ALEXA AND IOT

Some of our devices—and perhaps our house and car—will acquire simulated human voices. Moreover, there won't be the monotone of automatons like your GPS. Machines of the near future will cut through the ambiguity of human speech to converse with us in a way that will meet the requirements of the Turing Test—a **test** of a machine's ability to exhibit intelligent behavior equivalent to, or indistinguishable from, that of a human. *"The rub may be,"* as Jaron Lanier, who is considered a founding father of the field of virtual reality, wrote in his master polemic, *"You Are Not a Gadget, that the Turing test may cut both ways."*

You can't tell if a machine has gotten smarter or if you've just lowered your standards of intelligence to such a degree that it seems smart.

Our shorter attention span will be well-served media, although sites will be able to back up their reporting with an unprecedented depth of written, video and audio material that once would have been edited out and lost to posterity.

Another trend will be the blurring of media categories. If you follow *nytimes.com* or *abcnews.com* or your local TV, radio and newspaper websites, you will see in each case a combination of video, uploads, slide shows and text. As these media are more distant from their physical origins, the distinction between a newspaper, a radio show and a television show will be more a matter of emphasis and legacy.

Identity theft will remain rampant. You can expect the steady boil of personal and business cyber insecurity to continue; governments and large and small businesses will be assaulted by the wholesale theft and compromise of secrets by groups and their mirror sites that will be far more shadowy than WikiLeaks.

And I do not doubt that by the time this book makes its way to the list of classic marketing books (which this author hopes it will), more elephants would have entered this market war. But the question is, who will they be? Apple, Netflix, Tesla or someone unheard of.

*"It takes twenty years to build
a reputation and five minutes to ruin it.*

— **Warren Buffett**

Death of Privacy

At the end of his life, the great science-fiction writer, Arthur C. Clarke, collaborated with author Stephen Baxter to write a novel, *The Lijjot of Other Pays*. It was not a masterpiece as its characters were a bit thin. The plot was stuffed with filler scenes that don't amount to much. None of them kept the book from being a great read, because of the book's premise and startling theme.

In this futuristic novel, scientists develop an invisible microscopic wormhole camera that allows them to see what's happening anywhere on the earth. Over time, the technology will become as cheap and commoditized as cell phones. Soon anyone can open a wormhole to learn what anyone else is doing.

The result is the WikiLeaks vision taken to the EU and the immediate loss of all privacy. There is no discussion inside the White House, CIA, or any other or corporate entity in the world that cannot be seen and overheard before millions of people. There is no love affair, no payoff or bribe, no minor vice that can be performed without instant discovery and public observation.

After some years, the loss of privacy begins to alter the sense of what it means to be human. Some people walk around in the nude and shamelessly perform every bodily function imaginable in public. Others who once had shameful secrets to protect carry on as the before, only now without apology or shame. However, many people align with the standards of the society that is watching them, slavishly mugging for the cameras and making statements about virtue. In this novel, Robin Williams's Little Snitch finally makes the full transition to becoming Big Brother.

Citing a very clichéd example again. When George Orwell wrote his famous book *1984* way back in 1944, he had predicted all these things: How companies or governments will watch us at any point in time, reading our emotions, hearing what we say, understanding if we are saying anything against them. The same prediction had come true after 70 years when George wrote this book. So, George Orwell was a visionary, and he could see the future.

The same future, proved by WikiLeaks, became an international conspiracy, and Edward Snowden, who exposed the global surveillance program run by the USA, is still running for his life when he revealed all the details which US government was tracking. No, it's not just the US government, which is tracking all these details but also all the platforms which we use currently.

Again, as I say, we are not the consumers, we are the products they are using. Every aspect of our lives and even every mail we write is being tracked. And that's why Big Brother is not just watching us since 1984 when George Orwell spoke about it but is living with us, and we are making room for him to stay with us around the clock. Yes, I am not talking about anything else but that small 6-inch thing in your pocket which is called your smartphone. This smartphone is the biggest snitch we have. It tracks all your operation. It tracks where you go with it, who you are talking to and monitors all the applications and all your movements across the digital space.

A strange fact of the Internet, however, is that while it strips away from its victims, it readily bestows anonymity on the attackers. FaceConnect provides a partial answer by encouraging us to log on to third-party websites, mobile devices and gaining systems with our Face identity. If this is a trend, if everyone did go without a mask, the Internet would be a good thing.

The practices of consumer companies, which pay the highest dollar per user to collect and cognitive data mining, are beginning to monitor the less profitable areas of politics, public affairs, ideologies and nonprofits. You can take a look at the successful use of RapLeaf data in the recent **JotForm** initiative campaign.

Novelist Zadie Smith, in a tart New York review of the movie *The Social Network*, worries about the cultural impact of Facebook. *"When a human being becomes a set of a website like Facebook, he or she is reduced,"* Smith writes. *"Ever shrinks. Individual character, Friendships. Language. Sensibility. Away, it's a transcendent experience: we lose our bodies, our messages, feelings, our desires, our fears."* It reminds me that those of us who turn disgusted by what we consider an overinflated liberal-bourgeois sense of self should be careful what we wish for. Another debate will be about how the Internet defines deviancy down. How many of the 75 million monthly visitors to porn sites would have ventured into an adult bookstore a generation before?

Alternatively, how many of the millions who access adult dating sites would have so readily lost their virginity to strangers? If you find it difficult to give up your virginity to strangers, how can you, that too without any forethought, give up your privacy to strangers by sharing all the small details of your everyday life on social platforms. Why do you and others fail to protect their privacy like their virginity?

The greatest danger is that what now serves as a useful tool will become a crutch, and the crutch will atrophy those skills that make us most human.

Perhaps, the most critical response will be to adequately educate a generation of humans to use this technology from infancy. An immense promise in more profoundly integrating technology into teaching digital technology lets anyone climb the ladder by the wall by streaming courses and lectures online.

In a technological world, the killer apps will belong to the well-rounded, to the trustworthy, to those who can communicate well with customers or write a deft response online.

Above all, people who understand human behavior, based on the age-old motives of money, sex, power and envy, will still have the best grasp on things to come. This insight is needed as never before when our computers will have us relate to them by a familiar name. It will be a world of robots, androids and smart homes and cars.

Will technology degrade our culture or liberate it? Will it devalue individuals or magnify us? Will it foster so much mixed truth that we will lose our bearings? Will it be the most potent instrument in history for separating fact from fiction? When the day comes that the unseen computer behind our walls whispers a lie, will we have the presence of mind to keep our own counsel?

For most of us, our digital profile is our significant public profile and how that profile is perceived has a huge impact on our personal and professional lives. Perception can determine the fate of careers, reputations, products or businesses. That's why digital patterns are so important.

The painful truth is that we will never own our digital profile. The Internet owns it. However, this profile is within our power language.

Whether you are a corporate executive, manager, entrepreneur, restaurateur, doctor, lawyer, accountant, consultant, a singular sensation, or a team leader, celebrity, model or fashion designer, parent or grandparent, you must manage your reputation or else the Internet will do it for you.

Learning social media is like learning to play the piano. To be proficient at it, you need hands-on education, teaming through the actual keystrokes.

TIPS TO CHECK YOUR ONLINE IDENTITY

1. **Identity:** KnowEm is a site that can crawl the web to see if an evil clone is using your name or forms of online identity, or if a brandjacker has hijacked your business on social media.

2. **Boards:** BoardTracker, Boardreader, and Omgili are free services that catch a lot of what might be said about you or your subject on message boards and discussion threads.

3. **Social Media:** Google Blog Search is a good place to start with about what blogs are saying about your area. Social Mention can track what is being said on social networks like Facebook. IceRocket is another good blog search engine. Technorati indexes blogs and breaks them into helpful categories and perform searches. BlogPulse tracks blogging trends that might affect you. Addict-o-Matic, whose motto is "Inhale the web," can collate a load of material from across the social media universe.

4. **Business:** Yelp is the essential self-search for small or consumer business. Search sites specific to the sector, such as TripAdvisor, track online reviews of hotels. Use Radian6 and Alterian SMS to monitor social media conversations about your brand or product.

5. **News:** The Internet is rich with free searches from nations. If mentioned or quoted in a story, searches tend to be time sensitive. So be sure to use the correct time parameters if you are searching for news about yourself. To do a robust search, access Factiva or Nexis or explore local news outlets, many of which require payment.

6. **Images:** Google, Bing and Yahoo! image searches are often overlooked part of any search. Keep in mind to perform a reverse search on an image, idling who you are from an online photo.

When the initial attack occurs, first understand who is attacking you. Can you identify the attacker, or can you correlate his username with a profile or a blog?

Does the attack appear organic, going viral over community anger over your perceived misdeeds, or cruel humor at your expense? Alternatively, do you see the repetition of keywords and text that indicates that you may be the victim of a deliberate keyword stuffing?

Is there an organization behind this attack? If so, can donors be identified? Can the name of the organization give a clue to a possible hidden enemy who is subsidizing the attack?

If the above questions are answered, take the following steps:

1. If the offending material is on a third-party website, go to the page of that website containing the offensive material and e-mail the web host. Send them a polite request to remove the article. Explain why this information is inaccurate or harmful.

2. Don't let anger seep into the conversation. Don't make actions or threaten the webmaster. Use the age-old technique of counting one to ten before you say anything if you are angry and wait for an hour before replying to a mail when you are angry.

3. The same approach of sweet reason and appeals to fairness even extends to the actual attacker if they can be identified. A threat might egg them on. Some vicious people delight in entreaties, as

a predator might enjoy the squeals of his prey. If it seems, however, if the attack is based on a misunderstanding, politely set the attacker straight.

4. If the webmaster or actual attacker agrees to remove the post and they have not posted it on a major review site ask them to use Google's public URL Removal Tool to eventually wash it out as a cache copy or snippet in Google's search results.

5. Why are they attacking you? If this is a case of someone's unmixed truth against you and not a troll or a dedicated attack, try to entice the person who made the post into an offline conversation. Let him know how hurtful his remark has been, without expressing legitimate anger. However, while you are reasonable, collect as much information as possible. For example, be sure and capture their IP address from any emails. In many cases, however, a reasoned, civil approach can do the job.

6. Celebrities pay top dollar to separate fact from fiction and respond to rumors and lies that are spread about them. Find your equivalent. Don't post a response on a site where the message

board can make you the equivalent of the clown in the dunking booth. In clarifying the mixed truth, you may be forced to own up. Fully understand that a digital confession is forever. Will you make it worse by responding? If you have to explain some personal shortcoming context, at least make your statement on a site where you have some control.

In the running down of a rumor, follow the example of McDonald's, where they rebutted the ground-worm rumor by talking about the quality of its beef. In an online world, it is best not to repeat the graphic terms of the charge, otherwise, the offending keywords are boosted as search terms.

*"My Space is like a bar,
Facebook is like the BBQ
you have in your backyard
and LinkedIn is the office."*

— Reid Hoffman

Social Media Channels

Before we can go further into the book, we need to get familiarize with the popular social media channels, because each of them has their own rules that you should never break.

1. BLOG

The word 'blog' is a shortened form of the word 'weblog,' and it was first coined in the late 1990s. Blogs were initially thought of as simple online diaries. They were first written by individuals who memorialized their lives and pontificated on a number of subjects. They were esoteric in the early days, but then some clever technologist recreated easy-to-use blogging platforms like Blogger, Tumblr, WordPress, making it very simple for anyone to blog. Blogger was later purchased by Google, helping bring blogging to the masses.

A blog has genuinely helped democratize communication around the world. As many have quickly figured out, freedom of expression may be embraced by people who may not be happy with particular businesses or other people.

It surprises me that many professional people deliberately exert no control over their online reputations. While it's increasingly rare, I meet executives whose companies don't have websites. And many professionals proudly say that they aren't on Facebook or Twitter and don't pay much attention to their LinkedIn profiles. They believe that the less information about them online the better and this is often paired with the opinion that social media wastes time or is invasive. The strategy, if you can call it that, appears to be that they believe they can control what is said about them online by saying very little. They think that they can be 'off the grid.'

2. Facebook

1. A critical question to answer when making a Facebook profile is whether to use it primarily for business or personal use or perhaps for a combination of both.

2. To manage privacy controls, log into Facebook. In the upper hand corner is a tab 'Account' with a drop-down menu. Select 'privacy settings.' As of this writing, five options control who can see what information you share. I recommend using

a custom level to understand what bits of data may be entirely used and to choose whatever makes you comfortable.

Data Selfie tracks the Facebook activity of anyone who downloads it to show them how much of a trace they leave on the site. It then reveals how Facebook's machine learning algorithms employ that specific data to gain insights into the user's personality.

"The tool explores our relationship to the online data we leave behind as a result of media consumption and social networks—the information you share consciously and unconsciously," Data Selfie's website reads.

https://lifehacker.com/data-selfie-analyzes-your-facebook-usage-to-show-what-c-1792578083

3. One final note on Facebook is the Facebook Connect platform. You may have seen other websites that offer the option to log into them via Facebook Connect. You may inadvertently log into one of these websites using Facebook, and then whatever you do on that website

might be broadcast quite publicly. Actions like 'liking' a piece of content (for example, an article or video) or commenting would then be visible on that website and later reported back into Facebook, broadcast to your friends, and depending on your privacy settings, to the entire Internet.

4. Despite such risks, establishing a Facebook profile is a meaningful way that you can claim a brand identity online as well as creating communications that you control. If you haven't done so already, be sure to establish your vanity (or unique) Facebook URL by going to http://www.facebook.com/ username. This will allow you to claim the URL.

5. Facebook can easily enable evil clones because anybody can create a profile with any name and any picture. Those attacking from a Facebook page may not be who they say they are.

6. Likewise, someone can spoof a profile that pretends to be you. The latter is even more reason to claim your piece of a digital real estate to bolster credibility should you need to deny the validity of an imposter.

3. Twitter

Twitter is another potential source of consternation for online victims. Many popular personalities and companies have been spoofed on Twitter. One way that Twitter has responded to this is to establish a "Verified" account. For example, if you look at Superstar Shah Rukh Khan's Twitter page, https://twitter.com/iamsrk, the blue symbol indicates that his page legitimately represents the person it says it does.

https://twitter.com/iamsrk

The real power of Twitter comes alive in its integration with a myriad of third-party applications. These applications can help you search keywords mentioning yourself or your company, organize your followers into manageable groups, schedule tweets so that you can maintain digital activity during times in which you aren't literally in front of your Twitter-enabled smartphone.

I recommend checking out two services: TweetDeck (http://www.tweetdeck.com) and Hoot Suite (http://hootsuite.com). There are many alternatives to these, but going to their sites and understanding how they work provides a good primer.

4. SNAPCHAT

The mobile app Snapchat enables users to share photos videos via text message, but the catch is that they disappear after 30 seconds. Initially thought of as a smart way to erase a sexting trail, the company is a favorite for sending selfies, funny pics and videos, not just illegal stuff. With the ongoing fear that a foolish text might come back to haunt us, perhaps this is a way to avoid future reputation problems. With this in mind, it isn't astonishing that investors are enthusiastic about its myriad uses. In August 2014, Snapchat received another $20 million in venture capital on top of its other investments, bringing its value up to $10 billion.

Then there's GoTenna. This one is not an app but rather a personalized antenna that enables you to send text messages to another person who's equipped with the same device and located within a few miles. Advertising suggests it's a way to stay in touch while traveling in remote areas like a group of hikers staying connected in a nearby location without cell service. Marketers also say it's a way for friends at a crowded outdoor event, like a concert, to communicate if the mobile grid is overwhelmed. And according to GoTenna's website, *"Messages are end-to-end encrypted and not stored anywhere. They also can be set to self-exterminate once the recipient reads them."*

5. INSTAGRAM

Instagram is one of the best social media apps out there. Its simplicity is what makes it so great—it's just about photos, no status updates, no check-ins, nothing very complicated. But even though Instagram is simple and straightforward, there is still Instagram etiquette, and many people either don't know what it is or just choose not to follow it.

At the end of the day, you can do whatever you want with your Instagram profile. But just know that whatever you want to do might be annoying everyone who follows you—just saying. There are some people who will tell you not to post 20 selfies in a row, or stop posting pictures of your cat, or to make sure your #TBT photos are a legitimate throwback from at least ten years ago. I personally don't care about that stuff. I care about, well, you'll see. Here are 10 things you should never, ever do on Instagram because, seriously, you're driving everyone crazy.

Don't Use an Awkward Username

Unfortunately, the search function within Instagram isn't as powerful as other sites. If you make your username (and even your "real" name) hard to find, people won't be able to find and follow you. Instead, use the same username as your Twitter handle and make your name something easy to recognize, whether it's your real name or your business name.

Don't Set Your Profile to Private

Unless you are using Instagram solely for personal reasons and don't want to network, do NOT set your account to 'Private.' Instead, set your account to 'Public' so that new followers can see what you post and what you're about. You will gain followers much more quickly if they can see your content and don't have to wait for approval.

Don't Post Without a Caption

No matter how awesome your image is, it needs a caption. Posts with captions get higher levels of engagement, and they allow you to interact with your audience. Tell people what the photo is, share a quote and ask a question. Whatever it is, find something relevant to include on your posts.

Don't Overuse or Misuse Hashtags

Hashtags are extremely important on Instagram and should be used on every post to increase reach. However, using more than 7–10 hashtags is overkill. Choose 5–7 relevant hashtags to include in your caption. Don't use popular hashtags like #tagforlikes or #onedirection or #love if they have absolutely nothing to do with your post. Using inappropriate hashtags to show up in popular searches won't help you reach new followers—you'll actually end up alienating possible followers.

Don't Ignore Your Followers' Comments

When people take the time to comment on your posts or ask questions, do not ignore them! Make sure you check your notifications regularly to stay on top of comments. Then respond (using their @username to notify them) and thank them or answer their question. When used regularly, comments will significantly impact your relationship with your audience.

Don't Steal Other Instagram Users' Content

Just because you like someone else's photo doesn't mean you can post it as your own. If you want to utilize user-generated content (UGC) in your strategy, have users tag you or use hashtags on their posts. When reposting, always, always, always provide proper attribution. There are some third-party apps which will allow you to repost another user's post to your account while giving proper attribution to the original user.

Don't Crowd Your Posts Back-to-Back

If you have multiple images to share, don't post them one after the other on Instagram. Instead, space them out once every half an hour or an hour. Not only will this not crowd your followers' feeds but you'll get more engagement on each post if they're not redundant. Speaking of redundancy, you don't have to share five photos of the same thing. Pick one or two of the best images and share only those.

Don't Auto-Share Every Post to Facebook and Twitter

While I recommend sharing the occasional post to Facebook and Twitter, you don't want to share every post with your other sites. If you're always sharing every post on other sites, why would someone follow you on Instagram? Instead, share one photo and encourage your fans to come to see the rest of the images on Instagram.

Don't Follow Everyone Who Follows You

Just because someone followed you doesn't mean you have to follow them. Of course, if you find their content interesting or in line with what you want to see, follow them! Reciprocity is great. But don't feel obligated to follow everyone. If your Instagram feed is filled with images and content that you don't actually enjoy, you'll be less likely to use it.

TripAdvisor

TripAdvisor began as a travel-related search engine and was a portal owned by Expedia. According to the site's founder, the original intention was to connect the information available in travel guidebooks to individuals who were searching the web for their desired travel information.

TripAdvisor split from Expedia in 2011 and is now publicly traded on NASDAQ. The company has its fingers in many different pots, as it has built affiliations and made acquisitions of travel review sites around the globe. However, its core offering is segregated content in the form of ratings, reviews and photos—to the tune of about 350 million unique monthly visitors and 320 million reviews and opinions covering more than 6.2 million accommodations, restaurants, and attractions. TripAdvisor sites operate in markets worldwide.

TripAdvisor is easily accessed through its website but also has a mobile app for both smartphones and tablets. Many travelers use apps and mobile phones to research travel options.

Customers write reviews and their experience with the hotel, restaurant or attraction that they are overall patronizing matches the expectations for them.

TripAdvisor says that it will be reflected in the reviews. In fact, the company says that 93 percent of surveyed users have reported that their experiences mostly met the expectations set by the reviews.

TripAdvisor gives value to the regency, as the executives believe that more current experiences are worth to the site's visitors than a property's reputation from years earlier.

One of the best ways to protect your online reputation over the long haul is by increasing your existing online marketing efforts. By building your online profile with activities like blogging, applying for awards and telling authentic stories distributed through strong challenges, you can create your online firewall while also improving your sales and marketing activities. What does every great movie, book and marketing campaign have in common? The answer is a great story. Now, this may seem like an old mantra, but as Internet marketing dominated our agendas in recent years, we focused our energy heavily (and a bit too much in my opinion) on keywords, tags, short-form posts, tweets, etc. While it's okay to be brief in your communications, we can't let our story suffer because of the medium. And with the continued fragmentation of media, we need to return to telling stories because it sets our message apart and helps our meaning ring clear amid the cacophony in the marketplace.

Part of the beauty of the Internet is that its democratized market lets anyone write a blog that is easily searchable and findable. We can make our own videos, which can go viral and reach millions of eyeballs. The Internet is the world's most prominent open-for-business sign that has profoundly changed how we market.

But as the web has found its way as a tool, it has also influenced the way we communicate. For a period, to build awareness we were blasting out as much information as we could. Every Search Engine Optimization company would write press releases that said virtually nothing and distribute them to websites that published them. No story, no message, just keywords and gobbledygook, which somehow improved search results. The smart folks at Google figured it out and had since implemented ongoing changes that favor—yes, you guessed it right—original and meaningful content.

We need to return to telling our stories and engaging our audience with interesting information. The good news is that rather than being forced to develop thousands of pieces of nutrition-free content, you can be smarter about what you're distributing.

6. Wikipedia

Wikipedia entries are usually near the top of most search results. It is a radical experiment in human knowledge and crowd-sourcing that has mostly been successful. We have shown, however, that it is subject to abuse. Though Wikipedia's standards for Biographies of Living Persons (BLPs) have been tightened up since the attack on John Seigenthaler, it knows how to correct abuses when they occur. In May 2005, an anonymous editor posted a hoax article on Wikipedia about journalist John Seigenthaler. The article falsely stated that Seigenthaler had been a suspect in the assassinations of U.S. President John F. Kennedy and U.S. Attorney General Robert F. Kennedy.

1. Editing existing entries and responding to inaccuracies in editing makes Wikipedia entries is a tricky business, a task to be approached with caution. Do not assume that it will be a quick or painless process.

2. Whether you are making edits directly or engaging in dialog on the Talk Page, you should never create multiple Wikipedia accounts to inflate the apparent support for your efforts. Attempts at this sock puppetry can be quickly uncovered, causing a vicious boomerang.

3. The similar tactic of enlisting a friendly person to create accounts and weigh in on your behalf on Talk Pages, called meat puppetry its reputational risks. However, it is technically permissible and can lend to critical momentum.

4. Again this strategy, like every action within Wikipedia, is not a foolproof solution as you might find yourself unable to get an answer you ultimately want. Nevertheless, patience and calm persistence are called to building support and credibility, the ultimate currency in the Wiki economy.

Search Engine Optimization (SEO)

I still remember when in 1999, the first time I went to a cybercafé. We paid around Rs. 50 per hour for it. The moment I entered that cybercafé, it seemed like a very classy place quite unlike any other I'd seen in my life. The owner came with a small menu, and I was still thinking that it was a restaurant or that they were offering some snacks while we were surfing. But, interestingly, the menu was filled with multiple categories like cricket news, Bollywood, and you know what I am talking about.

You know why young boys used to go to the cybercafé back then. The world has completely changed now. I don't need to remember a website's name. I just need to know what I am talking about and I just need to go to Google and search for it. So, the world has completely changed in the last 20 years, and I am seeing a lot of more development happening as Alexa, and the voice searches continue to pick up whatever I ask for or request. So, I am very sure that in the near future, we won't need to even type on computers or our phones to talk about auto-search for something.

In the early days, to access web pages you had to have a certain amount of wherewithal: a computer with the right amount of firepower, a modem to access the web with your phone line, and the ability to acquire and install one of the Internet web browsers. Broadband and routers were years away, and nothing was that easy. If you were successful at aligning all the steps to get online, it didn't always work right.

Communication has been democratized, so anyone can say whatever he or she wants, whenever he or she wants. The downside is also that anyone can say whatever he or she wants, whenever he or she wants. The Internet is a double-edged sword.

The growth of social media, blogging platforms and complaint sites have made it all too easy to post negative information online. Using social media sites like Twitter, Facebook, YouTube, the general public regularly passes judgment on people and events. We have even begun to expect it. If a political candidate makes a misstep, for example, one of the first places we look for a reputation crisis is the social universe.

When you search for a person or company's name, Google or Bing uses a complicated algorithm to determine what links to display and in what order. You and potential character assassins can manipulate this algorithm for good or ill.

Reviews

A question-and-answer series conducted with brands and retailers, and that also surveyed consumers in 2014, published an interesting study. Among its findings are the following:

A **review** is an evaluation of a publication, service or company. They are essential for positive website ranking.

1. The top five factors that are impacting purchasing decisions are (1) price, (2) ratings and reviews, (3) reconfirm friends and family, (4) brand and (5) shipping and retailer.

2. Reviews have become a significant source of information for shoppers as a whopping 95 percent of consumers in the study reported consulting customer reviews. Of those shoppers, 24 percent consult reviews every purchase they make. For shoppers in the age group of 18–44 years, it jumps to 30 percent.

3. Consumers rely on the presence of negative reviews' authenticity and credibility.

4. Because consumers want to be confident in their purchases, the availability of product reviews is an import factor in their decision for big-ticket purchases such as electronics (82 percent), appliances (80 percent) and computers (80 percent).

5. 70 percent of mobile shoppers reported being more likely to purchase a product if the mobile site or app they're from has reviews.

6. Ratings and reviews have become table stakes, and brands and retailers can improve consumer experience reviews.

7. By making it easy for consumers to read and write reviews at home, in-store or on the go, brands and retailers increase traffic and conversations.

Keywords

One of the ways the search engine algorithms can be used in a forthright way for higher search results is by frequent but appropriate use of keywords in the copy on a website.

Monitoring Online Activity

Earlier, we discussed ways to assess your existing online profile. That, of course, is just the first step. You must protect yourself online by actively monitoring the Internet for potential threats. The Fortune 100 companies spend tens of thousands of dollars per month for robust online mini-reports. However, there are easy-to-use and free solutions for small business to establish an essential ability to keep tabs on the constant hum of the Internet.

Google Alerts

Go over to http://www.google.com/alerts, and you can enter any keyword of interest—and select a frequency by which be notified of new (or updated) websites that contain that keyword. This tool is an excellent way to easily stay up to date on what is being said about you or your company.

Social Mention

Like Google Alerts, Social Mention offers a similar service, but it tracks social networks and blogs. You can also sign up with them to receive alerts based on keywords of your choice at http://socialmention.com/-mull.

Domain Defense

Your domain is your base identity inside your website's URL or resource locator. All domain names are registered with a name and contact information of the owner, the administrative contact and technical contact. This information is publicly available for everyone on the Internet and can be easily searched for free. You can do so by logging on to http://www.whois.net.

The Whois Database

If a website is publishing negative and false information, then checking the Whois database is an excellent place to start. In some cases, you may not provide any means of communicating with them, so the Whois database can help you contact the owner. Also, it is possible that the owner of a website is unaware that there is negative information on their website about you. Smaller websites that may have been long since abandoned by their original owner are often easily hacked, and content can be uploaded onto their domain.

Domain Poaching

Another piece of information that is publicly available in the Whois database is when any domain was registered when it was last renewed and when it will expire. This data makes it easy for poachers to move in when domains are about to expire, and they can swoop in and purchase your domain. You need to prevent this from happening. The process is twofold: make sure that you have your domain registrar account set to auto-renew, and then make sure that your credit card or other payment information is up to date. Even if you have your domain set to auto-renew, if on the day the registrar attempts to charge your credit card only to have it bounce back that the card is expired, then domain poachers can capitalize on your mistake.

Domain Pirates

As the name suggests, domain pirates are precisely the pirates in the new digital and technology world. These pirates latch on and wait for famous domains to expire and then they capture the brand and ask them a tremendous amount of money to sell their domain. For a brand that is already established, there is no other way by which they can deny these domain pirates, and hence, they're left with no choice but to give them an amount of custody to get the domain back.

Please understand that these domain pirates are entirely different from domain brokers who keep the most famous domains they buy and keep them with them, and then they sell it when a brand is looking for a particular domain. These domain brokers are the people who latch on to a specific domain and invest money and time in it so when the right time comes they can sell it. As a personal piece of advice, I do think that domain brokers are people who've invested and it's like a stock market for they do invest that time and energy in finding out the right domain to sell it off and also, it's legalized practice currently.

"The best place to hide a dead body is page two of Google search results!"

— Search Engine Optimization proverb

Come to the Dark Side

DARK WEB, DEEP WEB AND SURFACE WEB

Darknet Is an Overlay Network—a network built on top of the Internet—which has been designed specifically for anonymity. It means that darknet is meant to be hidden. Two typical darknet types are friend-to-friend networks, and privacy networks such as Tor, I2P, Freenet, DN42, etc.

Now you may be confused about why I named the chapter 'Come to the Dark Side.'

Actually, darknet and dark web are related to each other. As mentioned already, darknet is a network built over Internet while term dark web refers to websites on a darknet. Dark webs are pages on servers that cannot be accessed by a search engine (or indeed, a user) without an appropriately authorized account. Large-scale illegal activities happen in dark web.

The Deep Web

Here's the easiest way to understand the Deep Web. It's all the data behind firewalls. You can think of user databases, business intranets, web archives, password-protected websites, etc.

By some estimates, this part of the Internet is estimated to be 400 to 500 times the size of the Surface web.

Sometimes you will hear the term Deep Web used interchangeably with Dark Web, but they aren't really the same thing.

1. Surface Web

Let me tell you one thing, if you bought this book legally from online then you explored the surface part of the web. But if you downloaded it from a torrent, then you actually traversed the deep web. The websites, web pages and information that you find using web search engine like Google, Yahoo, Bing, etc. Normal users are limited to using only the surface part of the web. The shocking fact is that the surface web is only 4% of the whole Internet!

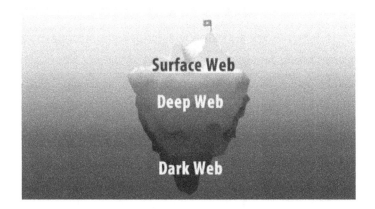

Dark Net

For some, 'dark net' means the encrypted world of Tor Hidden Services, where users cannot be traced, and cannot be identified. For others, it is the sites which are not indexed by conventional search engines, an unknowable realm of password-protected unlinked websites and hidden content accessible only to those in the know, sometimes referred to as the 'deep web.' It has also become a negative term for the myriad shocking, disturbing and controversial corners of the net, the realm of imagined criminals and predators of all shapes and sizes.

Because the Internet has become so interlinked into the fabric of our lives, it presents a challenge to our existing notions of anonymity, privacy, freedom and censorship, throwing up new challenges of finding out what is black and white. Are our "digital identities distinct from our "'real'–ones" and what does that mean? Are we supposed to behave in particular ways when we sit behind a screen? What are the limits of free expression in a world where every idea is a click away?

The Internet as we know started late in the 1960s, as a small project sponsored and run by the Advanced Research Projects Agency (ARPA), a research and development arm of the US military. Pentagon hoped to create an 'Arpanet' of linked computers to help top American academics share data sets and valuable computer space. In 1969, the first networked connection was made between two computers in California. It was a network that slowly grew.

Allow me to introduce you to some of the dark aspects of this mythical online world.

Trolling

Some form of trolling takes place on almost every online community like YouTube, Facebook and Twitter. All have their own kind of trolls, each evolved to fit their environment. Amateur pornography websites are populated with trolls who know precisely how to offend exhibitionists. The comment sections on reputable news sites are routinely bursting with insults.

'Trolling' has today become shorthand for any nasty or threatening online. However, there is much more to trolling than this. OhSoLame (Real name not disclosed for several unreasonable reasons) is in his early thirties and speaks with a soft Delhi accent. He has been trolling online users for over a decade now. Quoting his words, *"Trolling is not about bullying people. It is all about unlocking situations, creating new scenarios, pushing boundaries, trying ideas out, calculating the best way to provoke a reaction. Threatening to rape someone on Twitter is not trolling, that's just threatening to rape someone."*

Meeting the Trolls

Finding genuine trolls is difficult. Many use fake servers to mask their IP addresses, and most have dozens of accounts with different names for each platform they use. If they are banned or locked down by a particular site, they rejoin under a new name. However, like the Meowers (organized trolls), today's trolls enjoy spending time with other trolls. A lot of the worst trolling online is coordinated from hidden or secret channels and chat rooms.

The simplest way to deal with the trolls is to force websites or platforms to insist that their users interact and debate under their real names and remove the rest. That wouldn't stop online nastiness, but it would at least make trolls a little more for actions, and perhaps encourage them to leave anonymity online. Many trolls are merely bored teenagers trying to cause little trouble; the severe trolls seem to follow ideology broadly and believe that part of living in a free society is accepting that no idea is beyond being challenged or ridiculed and that nothing is more stifling to free expression than being afraid to upset or offend. Trolls have been in the system just as long as networked computing, which surely says something about the need many of us have to find the darker sides of our nature.

Whatever their motives, and even at their worst, perhaps we can learn something from trolls. Trolling is a broad party that has everyone from bullies to amateur philosophers, from the mildly offensive to the illegal. An increasing desire for digital affirmation is leading more of us to share our most intimate and personal lives often with complete strangers. What we like, what our thoughts are, what our sexual preference is, what our religious thoughts are, where we're going, everything is out there. The more we invest of ourselves online and the readier we are to be offended, the more there is for trolls to eat on. Despite the increased policing of social media sites, trolling is not going anywhere. It has been an innate culture of online life since the mid-1970s, evolving and mutating from an unexpected offshoot of electronic communication within a niche community to an almost-mainstream phenomenon.

If Twitter or Facebook trolls were available during the time of Mahabharata, I am very sure the massive destruction would not have happened and so many lives would have been saved. It would have been only a troll war between Kauravas and Pandavas and seeing the massive amount of Kaurav brothers, I am sure they would have won the war, and history would have been written differently.

Bitcoin

Bitcoin was launched to the world in 2009 via a public post on an exclusive mailing list for cryptographers. It quickly developed a following, and soon became the currency of choice for the online market Silk Road. A growing number of people started to exchange Bitcoin for dollars, which pushed its exchange rate. Currently (November 2018) it's trading at 251462 INR / Bitcoin.

Bitcoin's dramatic rise to prominence resulted in an explosion of investment, exchange companies and even ATMs. Most of the Bitcoin community has entered into complex negotiations with governments and regulators about how to make the new digital currency work alongside the traditional. The Bitcoin Foundation, a semi-official body that represents the currency, was established in 2012 to standardize the core development required to keep the system working securely and effectively. Although no one is really in charge of Bitcoin, the Foundation is probably the closest thing there is to a governing body. In 2013, the Bitcoin Foundation's annual conference was called The Future of Payment, a title that reflects the thoughts of many of its users: that Bitcoin could be the universal mode of payment. But not everyone agreed.

Deep Web and Online Reputation

The space of the Internet that everyone can see, indexed by search engines, is known as the surface web and sometimes called the clear or visible web.

Vast amounts of information and data are exchanged over search engines. Known as the deep web, it has dynamic web pages, blocked sites, unlinked sites, private (like those that require login credentials) and non-HTML content private networks. Amount of information on the deep web (also known as the low net, invisible web, hidden web) is 500 times greater than the surface web. Within the deep web resides another area of the Internet called the dark web (also known as the darknet), where individuals can exchange info anonymously, and often do so nefariously.

Most frequently, people compare the Internet to an iceberg and describe the surface web as the ice above the water and the deep web as the 90 percent of the ice you can't see beneath the waterline. On the deep web and dark web can have an actual impact on online reputation, so it's important to understand the differences.

Individuals use the dark web to navigate anonymously. While some privacy advocates say it is right not to be tracked online, others say it's fair. On the dark web, individuals can find sources of illegal drugs, counterfeit money, weapons, leaked documents and child pornography among other illicit things. It is also used by underground dissidents, and whistleblowers—and journalists who wish to communicate with them. Law enforcement and government agencies also search the dark web to track criminals and terrorists.

It can be a scary place.

Access to the dark web requires a unique web browser, of which are several. You can't get there from the search bar on Chrome, Safari, Internet Explorer or Firefox. So, don't worry that you will find their way into it while playing games on an iPad. But what about your children? That's another story.

One of the most well-known browsers for the dark web is called 'The Onion Router' as its many layers of encryptions that are akin to an onion. Today it is just called Tor; it serves as an open-source software program that allows users to protect their privacy and security. Ironically, Tor was originally developed for the US Navy as a way to protect government communications. It is made up of a group of volunteer-operated servers that enable people to communicate privately and confidentially using a series of virtual tunnels and connections. On its website, Tor bills itself as a tool with many above-board uses.

1. Individuals use it as active censorship circumvention, a mechanism for maintaining civil liberties and a place for socially sensitive communication: rooms and web forums for crime and abuse survivors and people with illnesses.

2. Journalists use Tor to communicate more safely with whistleblowers and dissidents.

3. Non-governmental organizations use it to enable their workers to connect to their home website while they are in a foreign country to keep their location a secret.

4. Corporations use it as a safe way to conduct competitive analysis and to protect sensitive communications from eavesdroppers.

5. Law enforcement uses Tor for visiting or surveying without revealing government IP addresses and security during sting operations.

Silk Road

The Silk Road was an ancient network of trade routes that connected the East and West. It was central to cultural interaction between the regions for many centuries. This was the original Silk Road. It helped in booming the culture and economy of east and west. In the same way, the Internet has transformed commerce and trade. It seamlessly connects buyers and sellers around the world, opens new markets and makes shopping simple, convenient and quick. Approximately 50 percent of all global consumers now make online purchases, a percentage that grows every year. However, alongside the multi-billion-dollar world of e-commerce, with its buy-it-nows, one-click and next-day deliveries, exists another market that is proliferating. In this world, everything, legal and illegal, is for sale.

Technology is often described as 'neutral.' However, it could be more accurately described as power and freedom.

The darknet is a world of power and freedom, of expression, of creativity, of information, of ideas. Power and liberty endow our creative and destructive faculties. The darknet magnifies both by making it easier to explore every desire, to act on every impulse and every neurosis.

Hidden encrypted websites and mysterious underground drugs markets sound like they exist far below the world of Google and Facebook. But cyberspace doesn't have depth. If you know where to look, everything is accessible. In the darknet, we can find more, do more and see more. Moreover, in the darknet, we have to be careful, cautious and responsible.

The darknet fosters breathtaking creativity. Most of the sites I visited were astonishingly adaptive and innovative. Outsiders, radicals, and pariahs are often technology adept in ingenious ways, and the rest of us have much to learn from them.

Each responds differently to the power and freedom that any technology creates.

"Our reputation is more important than the last hundred million dollars."

— Rupert Murdoch

How to Protect Your Own and Your Brand's Identity and Reputation

The Internet is changing and shifting at such a rapid rate that new opportunities to attack people online will continue to emerge, so we mainly have to tackle today's issues while waiting on and trying to anticipate the next wrinkle.

PROTECTING YOUR REPUTATION BEFORE APPLYING FOR A JOB

Employers may instantly check credentials by using Google searches, and they're looking for a lot more than proof of matriculation. I have fielded dozens of calls from individuals, both young and old, who have had problems getting jobs due to online issues.

If you're applying for a job, it's best to assume that prospective employers will be checking you out online. You will be Googled.

Because the Internet is now the king, we are in a whole new world of crisis management. More and more situations arise where people are literally in the wrong place at the wrong time and end up crucified online. They will find themselves in a massive problem that they are in no position to solve.

An important thing to understand is that yesterday's public relations strategies aren't sufficient to combat the damage done by the Internet.

When we encounter a crisis, we need to quickly determine what the online legacy will be and then formulate a strategy to prevent negative coverage from the onset. Understanding that the chances of something stated online (whether true or not) becoming damning for years to come is critical.

Negative online articles and stories can be mitigated and, in some instances, completely removed, but this process is expensive and not always possible. The big lesson is that if you are associated with something negative, either directly or indirectly, or just by accident, the online reporting of it can affect you for years to come. The problem must be managed as quickly and aggressively as possible.

Companies can do dumb things too. In April, a public relations person at US Airways responded to a routine flyer with a tweet. The tweet said, "We welcome feedback, Elle. If your travel is complete, you can detail it here for review and follow up." The tweet included a link. Through some malicious scheme, the link led to an obscene clip of a woman pleasuring herself with a model jet airplane. It took almost 60 minutes before the company removed the tweet, and by the time it had blazed a trail through the Internet.

The company sent out a tweet after the original image which garnered more than 500 retweets. "We apologize for an inappropriate message recently shared as a link in one of our responses. We have the tweet and are investigating."

By that time, it had been called "the worst tweet in the history of Twitter." How did it happen? No one knows for sure, but one scenario is that a hacker exploited a security vulnerability of the airways' Twitter password and posted the picture as an act of malice. 'Do bad tweets last forever?' Just Google 'US Airways tweet' and see for yourself.

How a Single Social Media Event Can Ruin the Career of a Politician

A young politician who is the head of one of the biggest political parties in India did one single interview in which they were few cuts which were taken and were played on social media. This whole interview just completely ruined the career of this particular young man and he is still seeing the results of that one interview. I am not saying that people don't make mistakes, but on social media, people can pick up any particular word and turn it into a story. It becomes effortless to reproduce that kind of content and to make calls to the same somebody on social media.

Some people are using our newly democratized communication to practice online extremism. Consider how simple it is to create an anonymous and practically untraceable hate blog. Anyone can do it in three easy steps.

1. Secure a nondescript e-mail address on websites like Google, Yahoo or AOL.

2. Use that e-mail address to create a blog on a site like Blogger or Tumblr.

3. Start writing malicious content about your chosen victim.

Within no time, the posts can start appearing high on search results, particularly if the victim doesn't have a strong online reputation. If the perpetrator is smart and mean enough, he or she can cause immense reputational damage and even the professional or personal life of the victim can be harmed. A similar strategy is employed to attack a business using an online complaint, and again, the perpetrator can be anonymous and hidden.

Technology hasn't made us meaner, but it is now much easier to be mean.

PERSONAL REPUTATION MANAGEMENT
People Being Victimized

Personal Reputation Damage can do more damage to the online reputation of a person or organization than a hate blog. Often created anonymously and sometimes by very web-savvy individuals, a negative blog can do immense damage to someone.

The year 2017 was a shocking year for the Indian content industry as one of the most significant leaders of the industry, Arnab Kumar, CEO of The Viral Fever, was accused of sexual harassment by an anonymous blog posted on social media that went viral.

Sexual harassment in India has always been a big issue. Whenever you see a sexual harassment case against a male, we assume that the harassment case is always right. Now, I am not debating about any sexual harassment case in particular, but the point I want to make is that social media has made it so easy to talk about sexual harassment by any public figure, anonymously. Quite a few people readily agree to the women who are making the allegations but don't think twice before pointing fingers at the men. They don't even listen to the person who has been accused of such crimes. This is an unfortunate state of affairs currently in which anonymously somebody can blame somebody and the whole world accepts it as the truth.

This concept of authority is critical when one is dealing with online reputation situations. Your profiles on Facebook and Twitter usually outperform your company's site on Google searches.

Most of us know that we can switch off web browser settings that track our history. Private browsing makes sense when you're using someone else's computer, want to view pages without historical cookies influencing the act of performance, or want to keep your web activity private. Almost 1 in 2 users opts for private browsing.

https://blog.globalwebindex.com/chart-of-the-day/
almost-1-in-2-use-private-browsing-windows/

If you are to make profound emotional statements on Facebook, it's best to not include your work colleagues within your Facebook sphere. If you are very political, which is fine by the way, it's probably best not to add in your network those people who vehemently disagree with you.

I know one of the ex-CEOs of a very big agency in India who has been very, very open about his political intonation and talks about it in articles and videos that he writes and shares. There is this another gentleman, who is in his friends list, again a very reputed person in the digital marketing arena, who keeps responding to his comments, and these immature adults above 45 fight like kids on social media about political parties.

No, I am not against somebody or a strong supporter of a political party. However, I definitely suggest for an online reputation point of view that you should keep it with yourself. Even if you are promoting, at least don't get into these heated discussions and string into each other on a social media platform because it's not just about your image, it's also about the reputation which you have built from such a long time, and it can get ruined just because of silly remarks.

Take Control of Your Online Reputation

If someone is looking for information about you, he or she will do it online—I promise. Everyone has left digital breadcrumbs somewhere. The Internet may find kind things like property listings in old newspaper clippings, or corporate filings. However, it is content like arrest reports, lawsuits and negative reviews blog posts that are rampant. If you don't take control of your online reputation, ignore your digital image at your own peril.

Here are a few simple steps you can do to protect your online REPUTATION:

Build your social profile.

Ultimately, when hackers are checking you out online, they want to find the most relevant information. Taking control of your online profile by populating the Internet with positive news is good. Here are four quick ways to take control of results:

1. Create your website (try to get your name as the URL) and post your resume there.

2. Get a LinkedIn account with your photo, current education and job history posted.

3. Create a Twitter account with a name in it, and post business-related content.

4. Secure a Facebook page with your real name and complete your profile. Unlike regular Facebook accounts that are closed to Google searches, Facebook Pages (the company capitalizes the term) are public and searchable.

Google yourself every once in a while. See how the most potent digital front door perceives you so you can react if something goes wrong or something weird happens.

Follow the rules.

Control your content. This might seem obvious, but don't post if you can't control. Delete or 'untag' any embarrassing or inappropriate pictures posts. The last thing you would need is a sloshed night from years ago costing you a chance to land your first job. Even after your first job out of college, you shouldn't forget about your online reputation.

Respect one another and respect yourself.

Be proactive, not reactive. Prospective employers will likely Google your name and see what comes up. Cleaning up your reputation begins with seeing if it needs to be cleaned up in the first place.

Apart from the embarrassing content that may be on the phone itself, if you genuinely want to protect yourself from the many dangers of a stolen phone, you need to have everything of value backed up preferably, automatically. If you lose custody of your phone, the physical value of your phone should be the only concern you have.

PICTURES AND MUSIC

If you take many notes on your phone, make sure they are backed up or use one of the cloud-based note services like Evernote. If your cell phone disappears, then all you need do is change your password, and your notes are SAFE.

THE PASSCODE ON PHONE

I will admit that I didn't use the passcode feature initially on my iPhone, but now it is a necessity. If you have to enter a four-digit code to access your phone, it is a safe option. Each time you open it or after your phone been idle for a set amount of time, up to one hour, you're asked to enter it. There are ten thousand possible codes, so it is not easily hacked unless you chose the lazy path and used silly and easy passcodes like 1234, 0000 or your birth year. Use a passcode that is unique.

UNPROFESSIONAL BEHAVIOR

Unprofessional behavior online keeps you from getting hired. Think about it, if someone from HR is trying to decide whether or not you'd be a good fit for their company, they need to make sure that there's no visible evidence that you're unprofessional. If there is information out there that suggests this, then they're liable if you repeat that sort of action once hired. 'Unprofessional' can mean a variety of different things depending on whom you ask.

There are some prominent examples of unprofessional behavior like publicly complaining about co-workers, bosses, past employers, etc. However, other practices may not be quite as evident to some. For example, mentions of skipping or showing up late for school or work can come off as extremely unprofessional, even if these kinds of comments are just said in jest. Additionally, if you post online about something that you did when you should have been at work or school, you're flaunting that you lied, and don't care about your job or school. Demonstrating that you don't care about your education or career (with your words, original posts or shared content) is extremely unprofessional. Not only will this adversely impact your Reputation Score, but future employers will take note of this and any other behavior that could be perceived as questionable in the workplace.

2. Unprofessional Communication Style

Whether you're trying to win clients or get into your dream college, how you communicate can have a severe effect on the outcome of your online screening (and your Reputation Score). At BrandYourself, we want to make sure that our clients and subscribers have the best chance at succeeding at their goals.

Moreover, according to our research, 'unprofessional communication style' is a surprisingly common reason why people get rejected after undergoing an online screening. It's easy to overlook this when posting or commenting on your social media—when you're talking to your friends. Unfortunately, that relaxed attitude can hurt when it comes time for any essential online screenings. Use of swear words or profanity is quickly flagged as a potential deal-breaker.

And poor grammar or spelling also incites concern since 'professional communication' is integral in so many work environments. So, the next time you post something, imagine that a future boss is trying to decide whether or not you have a 'demonstrated ability to communicate effectively in professional settings.'

3. Drinking or Drug Use

While there are of course some exceptions to this (if you're a sommelier and took pictures during a company wine-tasting trip to a vineyard), it's best to avoid sharing content that features you drinking or engaging in recreational drug use.

Again, some pictures (sipping a glass of wine on vacation) may be relatively tame, but even those can get you fired based on your job.

Avoid posting photos of chugging a beer, making keg stands, recklessly partying or anything else that would make your mother cringe. Even if you weren't entirely wasted when the photos were taken, you're effectively guilty by association in the eyes of anyone screening you.

And when it comes to drugs or illegal substance, avoid posting pictures, videos, comments, song lyrics, other things, etc. that refer to this kind of lifestyle. This applies to illicit drugs or prescription drugs. Either way, your future employers will likely red flag this sort of content, and your Reputation Score will take a hit.

4. Criminal Behavior

While this may seem pretty straightforward, it bears repeating when considering your Reputation Score and job prospects. Avoid posting, sharing or making any comments that suggest an admission of guilt of illegal behavior or activity. Even if you don't say something explicitly, there are typically enough context clues that aren't that hard to fill in if someone is scrutinizing your online presence.

People often run into trouble with this when alluding to underage drinking, taking drugs and "pranks." Things that are often labeled as "pranks" online are just misdemeanors—or even felonies, depending on the situation.

Refrain from the admission of any illegal behavior like shoplifting, breaking, theft, vandalism, etc.

5. Polarizing Views

This can be a bit tricky depending on how outspoken you like to be, where you work and what you do. However, typically, we suggest that users avoid making extreme statements about hot topics like religion, politics, etc. The reason we say this is because most people who have extreme viewpoints (especially if they don't align with the values of your potential employer) are flagged.

Also, you may not be able to walk back polarizing statements you share publicly today if your views change in the future. Additionally, many nuances can be lost online, and something you discussed with friends in real life over a 4-hour dinner may not translate to a 140-character tweet. Furthermore, you may not want to lead with your most controversial views when applying for jobs. In other cases, polarizing views may be unavoidable. For example, if you are a politician or social activist, there's a good chance that some of your opinions are polarizing.

So choose whether or not to take up extreme positions on controversial current events and issues based on your particular situation. Moreover, remember that this can impact your Reputation Score.

6. Sexually Explicit Content

Unless you work in an industry that encourages a frank discussion about sex (sex education, sex therapy or adult entertainment), avoid sexually explicit content at all costs. This includes posting about sexual behavior, genitals, porn, etc. And avoid posting sexually provocative photos or videos.

Make a point to avoid any other sexually charged content that could make someone feel uncomfortable. Again, HR will pay particular attention to this kind of content as a potential liability—as will your Reputation Score. So why risk it, especially if it has no relevance to your professional life?

7. Violence or Bullying

At baseline, employers are interested in cultivating a safe work environment that lets employees be as efficient at their jobs as possible. Most employees take a zero-tolerance approach to anyone who ruins that with the threat of violence or bullying. Not only does it reduce productivity in employees and sour the company culture, but it's also a huge liability. Employers can't knowingly hire people who demonstrate these kinds of attitudes or behaviors. This means that you should avoid using hateful speech online. And never hurl offensive insults or threats online. Even if this was empty, taken out of context or 'just a joke,' employers will look at it as a red flag reason to not hire you.

There are other subtler examples of this kind of behavior like photos or footage of you giving the middle finger or flashing other lewd gestures. Even if you were kidding around with friends when this was taken, this type of content can reduce your Reputation Score and ruin your chances at landing that job. Another behavior that employers are very sensitive to is people who talk excessively about using weapons, showing off their armory, or threatening/fantasizing about hurting others with real or imagined threats.

8. Bigoted Behavior

When it comes to screening you online, the person looking you up online will immediately be turned off by examples of bigoted behavior. Discriminatory remarks toward race, gender, religion, country of origin, sexual orientation or any other indication of intolerance toward groups of people will not serve you. This is a huge red flag. Not only does it show that you will create an uncomfortable or unsafe environment at work, but you are also a walking liability. If anyone of your co-workers or an external source discovers your online presence, your employer's reputation will also suffer.

And if you don't view yourself as a bigoted person, reconsider what it is that you're posting, sharing and how you're engaging online. Maybe certain things that you consider to be jokes are hurtful and offensive to other people. Alternatively, perhaps something isn't getting appropriately translated through the online medium.

Avoid the red flags listed above, because these are the behaviors most likely to get you booted from consideration for your next professional opportunity and decrease your Reputation Score. More importantly, if you notice any trends when reviewing your online presence (like you only post about your sword collection, you have to delete 50 pictures of you drinking straight bottles of whiskey, or post much-bigoted content) take some time to reflect on this. Is that who you are? Do you have a problem that you need to get help for? Do you need to diversify what you post about? Whatever it is, make a note of this as it will help determine the direction of your branding strategy going forward. It may also help you grow as a person.

Increase your Reputation Score and professional prospects with positive reinforcing factors

Actively building your brand is a must if you want a better Reputation Score and to land that next professional opportunity. Getting rid of damaging search results is only part of the process of improving your Google Reputation Score and social Reputation Scores. And remember, there's no need to dwell on harmful content about you that you can't control. Focus on accentuating the positive, and building up the assets that make up your brand.

During this building phase, you need to cultivate a brand that demonstrates positive reinforcing factors. In addition to researching what online factors instantly discourage employers from hiring people, our developers examined content that attracts employers. After scouring through existing studies, reviewing trends in our user-generated data and more—we've identified the most critical positive reinforcing factors.

While the following list does not include everything that you can do to increase the likelihood of an employer hiring you or a college accepting you, this is the most effective place to start.

1. Concrete Examples of Your Professional Behavior

Just as unprofessional behavior is a top red flag, clear examples of your professionalism make you a more desirable candidate. So how exactly can you show professionalism when building your brand? There are very concrete ways to show the caliber of your professionalism, but there are also more subtle ways that your brand can demonstrate this too.

Regarding the apparent examples, make sure to highlight your leadership experience and skills. Whether you stepped up to lead your team at work when your supervisor was ill, headed a professional development group with co-workers or have demonstrated leadership skills outside of the office—showcase it. In addition to making sure that you feature this in your bio and on your LinkedIn account, work to incorporate this into your content strategy if possible. Share the most recent presentation you made to your group of mentees, write a post about what it felt like to take on more responsibility, start a Facebook group dedicated to your professional development pursuits. What's most important is that you share this side of yourself with the people who are screening you online.

While mentioned briefly above, remember that LinkedIn is the go-to professional networking site.

That means it's in your best interest to pay particular attention to keeping your presence there up to date, active and thoughtful and polished (according to a small study). By focusing your efforts on how you look on LinkedIn, you have a great platform to highlight your strengths and experiences with leadership.

In addition to incorporating your leadership activities into your social presence, and staying active on LinkedIn, you've also go to present any awards or recognition that you've received. This serves as an additional form of validation that showcases you behave professionally behavior.

And don't forget to include descriptions of yourself, your skills, your past experiences and your future goals in ways that directly relate to the qualifications necessary for the job you're applying for. This shows that you are not only capable of the job, but that you also did your homework and highlighted what will work best for this future employer. This makes the review process much easier for the hiring manager. It will also increase your social Reputation Score, Google Reputation Score and overall Reputation Score.

2. Ability to Communicate Professionally

While we touched on what unprofessional communication looks like in the red flags section, let's consider what it looks like to communicate professionally—according to hiring officers and employers. When a potential employer looks you up online, they want to find language that is free of spelling & grammatical errors. They're looking for a style that is appropriate for the workplace. However, most importantly, they want proof that you are invested in your industry. This facet of professional communication means that you are writing, posting and sharing information that is relevant to your industry. It doesn't matter if you work in real estate, academia, auto-body repair or hedge funds. The point is that the content of what you share online should reflect some aspect of your professional life.

3. Professional Images, Photos and Videos

When vetting potential hires, employers need to know that the photos connected to your name are appropriate for work. Images and videos should reinforce your professional pursuits. So, make sure to take pictures of that panel you spoke on, or at that conference you attended.

Demonstrate that you commit some of your free time to independently developing yourself as a professional and growing your network. However, you're not a robot. Hiring managers also want to see images that tell them about your hobbies. You are a human after all, and potential employers want to learn more about your interests and who you are. So make sure to incorporate evidence of the things that make you YOU!

4. *Appropriate Online Engagement*

Hiring managers want to find the best candidate for the job who also fits well with the company's culture. So, when they look you up online, they are looking for evidence that you are this person. They aren't just looking for reasons to reject you!

The way that you choose to engage online can persuade a hiring manager to reject you flat out or can convince them to hire you. That's why engaging online in a way that shows that you're interested in what you do, have hobbies and common sense about what is and is not appropriate can potentially determine whether or not you land a job.

"As a business leader somewhat in the spotlight, it is impossible to hide."

— Cédric Manara

What to Do If It Happens to You?

When confronted with harmful online content that hinders your business or damages your reputation, the best advice is to keep calm and make a good assessment. While the first reaction may be to blast away at the hate blog, defamatory post, negative or nasty review, we have found that it makes more sense to go down and develop a strategy before confronting the source assuming you can figure out who posted the negative information in the first place.

You have the right to remain silent. Though silence can be a huge mistake when dealing with a traditional public relations crisis, with these issues, it can be a prudent strategy. An impetuous response to the negative search result may add credibility to untrue allegations and fuel the fire of a renegade blogger.

Is it removed? Contrary to popular belief, you can remove the negative Google search results. It's not always possible, but there are situations when it can be done.

Violations of Terms and Conditions on Blogging Platforms

Here is what the majority of blog platforms do not allow their users to post:

1. ADULT CONTENT

2. EXPLOITATION OF CHILDREN

3. HATE SPEECH

4. CRUDE CONTENT

5. HARASSMENT

6. COPYRIGHT INFRINGEMENT

7. PERSONAL AND CONFIDENTIAL INFORMATION

8. IMPERSONATION OF OTHERS

Different blog platforms offer different ways of reporting content that is harmful or abusive.

Listed below are links to the terms of writing content and how to report it for three major blog platforms:

Blogger service:

www.blogger.com/contentg How to publish content: to report content on Blogger, visit http://support.google.

com/blogger/amwer/76315?M' and select the abuse type to access the relevant contact form

Tumblr of service:

www.tumblr.com/policy/en/terms_oj_service to report content: e-mail abuse@tumblr.com

WordPress:

Terms of service: http://en.wordpress.com/tos How to report content: for logged-in WordPress users report content, use the "report this content button located underneath the blog menu on the toolbar. Me blog menu on the voodoo-the fagged-in WordPress user you can us*f found here: http://en.wordpress.com/abuse

When you research online reputation management websites, you quickly learn that they offer a distinct service known in the industry as suppression. Online reputation companies create new content with the hopes of pushing down or suppressing negative search results. This tactic can be very selective, but it isn't the best solution or the most economical—though the prices are dropping.

Information is not removed from search results, instead pushed further down the search result pages to a point where fewer people will see it.

When individuals search for information online, they rarely go beyond the first few pages of search results. So, if a negative item is, for example, on page three or beyond, only a fraction of folks online will see it. Some studies have been completed regarding this, and while the methodologies are different and the results vary, I can confidently tell you that the majority of people looking for information don't get past page three. A study published on the Marketing Land website in 2014 suggests that the first five listings on page one alone get more than 65 percent of clicks.

Today, there are dozens of companies that offer online reputation management services. For many, even those within the tech industry, the terms online reputation management and online content suppression are the same thing. This industry has grown in the past several years,

This may include creating blog sites and microsites on your behalf and also generating new content to populate the many new pages. And the strategy works in some cases, as negative information pushed from page one, and the client is happy that the negative content is only found in the most definitive of searches.

CASE STUDY FOR A POLITICIAN –
SEX SCANDAL

One of our clients, a reputed son of a politician came to us. He was planning to run for elections next year, but someone in a sex scandal case falsely accused him.

When you searched his name on Google, nearly half of the first page of results mentioned the police sting and his alleged association with the misdeed. Because the incident was reported on several news sites, including that of a major daily newspaper, I knew that it would be difficult to negotiate the direct removal of the results. High-authority sites like major newspapers are also outside the realm of even the expensive covert operations guys. We decided on suppression and mounted a campaign to flood the Internet with positive information about him that would push down the negative news.

First, we tackled the major social media sites, ensuring that he had a complete profile on Facebook, Twitter, LinkedIn, and Google+. Search engines like Google, Yahoo, and Bing view sites like these as high-authority providers' information, and they typically dominate the first pages of search results for individuals.

Next, we created a vanity site for him, purchasing his name as the URL and populating the site with business and personal information. Remember that Google and the other search engines want to send users to the best post sources regarding a search term, so claiming his full name as a website URL, and then adding real information about him, created a robust digital asset. Besides, we created other digital content on his behalf, including videos, which were posted on sites like YouTube and Vimeo, and images posted on sites like Pinterest.

Over the next several months, we consistently posted new information to his social media sites, his vanity site and to other places on the web. He began to see results within the first month of our suppression campaign as his Facebook, Twitter and LinkedIn accounts worked their way up to page one of search results, which in turn started to push down the negative stories.

It took some time, about three months in total, but we eventually gained control of 90 percent of the search results for his name on the first page of Google results, and we eliminated any mention of his arrest when you searched the first four pages of results on both

Yahoo and Bing. As of this writing, while anyone who is genuinely digging for dirt on this politician will be able to find information about his arrest, the casual web surfer is more likely to see positive or benign content about him.

The results we secured for him are fairly typical of a suppression campaign. We didn't eliminate any negative content, but we were able to push it down to pages that most folks never reach. We weren't able to completely clean up his online results, but we improved his online profile enough so that he can lead his life as a productive and responsible citizen.

'Cyberbullying and Cyberstalking'

Often used interchangeably by the media, cyberbullying and cyberstalking are terms that typically refer to situations where someone uses the Internet or other electronic means to stalk or harass an individual, group or organization. Cyberstalking is considered cyberbullying. It may also include threats, vandalism, identity theft, monitoring, and real-time, in-person stalking. Regardless if it is online or offline, stalking is considered a form of mental assault and is a criminal offense.

Cyberbullying, more frequently associated with children and teens, is bullying that takes place using electronic technology such as smartphones and computers as well as social media sites. In my opinion, anyone who believes or their loved ones are a victim of cyberbullying or cyberstalking should contact the police immediately.

While some may still view the Internet as the Wild Wild West, Google and the other major search engines have made efforts to remove some online content that has little redeeming value or can cause significant damage.

"Our philosophy has always been that search should reflect the whole web," Amit Singhal, Senior Vice President of Google Search, said in a blog post at the time. *"But revenge porn images are impersonal and emotionally damaging and serve only to degrade the victim—predominantly women."*

Monitoring social media channels enables a business to track online reputation issues as they happen. This knowledge can help avert a crisis. While many of us will probably be okay with checking our social media feeds daily, or even frequently, some organizations are better served with real time, at least a systemized approach that alerts them of online brush fires.

Monitoring represents the first step toward online engagement, and it proves useful for both customer service and reputation management. Knowing what people are saying as soon as possible, offers the options for engagement and response.

Such systems can then compare and contrast your organization's activity with that of your competitors and determine performance. It has a more significant share of social media or traditional media. So-called share of voice reports can help you judge the effectiveness of your marketing efforts against those of competitors.

HOW FAKE NEWS IMPACTS THE STOCK MARKET

Then – 1814

On Feb. 21, 1814, a man in uniform purporting to be Col. R. du Bourg, an aide to Britain's ambassador to Russia, arrived at the Ship Inn in Dover, England, claiming that French Emperor Napoleon Bonaparte had been killed by Russian Cossacks. The man sent a horse and rider to bring the news to Adm. Thomas Foley, who decided to relay the message to the Admiralty in London by semaphore telegraph system but couldn't because there was too much fog. The man claiming to be du Bourg, meanwhile, set out for London, stopping at every inn along the way to spread the news.

Meanwhile, three men dressed as French officers distributed leaflets in London announcing that Napoleon had been killed. The news sent the price of government securities on the London Stock Exchange soaring until it turned out that Napoleon was still very much alive.

An investigation by the exchange found that there had been a recent large purchase of government-based stocks, and charged three people with fraud. One was Lord Thomas Cochrane, a Member of Parliament and naval hero. The conspirators were sentenced to 12 months of prison time and a fine. Lord Cochrane continued to assert his innocence and was later granted a pardon.

Now – 2013

A press release from Fingerprint Cards, a publicly-listed Swedish company, said it would be acquired by Samsung for $650 million, well above Fingerprint's market cap of $420 million. Fingerprint's stock soared by over 50% in a matter of minutes, adding $200 million to its valuation. The narrative sounds believable enough—Apple recently introduced fingerprint sensors in its new iPhone, and if Samsung wanted to catch up in a hurry, buying a company that already makes the technology would be the fastest way to do it. It seemed almost too good to be true.

It was. A baffled Samsung denied any talk of a takeover, a now-deleted press release on Fingerprint's website notwithstanding. Cision, the company that handles Fingerprint's press releases, called the release "completely false" and said it is investigating the release.

These cases prove that fake news is not a new phenomenon. It has been around since ancient times, but only now, it is on steroids. Now, instead of traveling on waggling tongues it spreads by riding on the impulsive fingers and ill-informed tweets.

As I said earlier also, the Internet has not made us meaner, it has just made the ways to be mean and corrupt a bit easy.

Monitoring service Capifeo creates reports of media and online activity as it relates to your entire industry, helping a company's executives stay abreast of the latest industry news. In fact, services work in conjunction with existing media databases so articles can be viewed and read even if they need to be paid to be viewed or are posted on sites that require a subscription. This by itself is valuable as many Google searches can pull up news articles that can't be viewed in their entirety without a subscription.

Comprehensive online monitoring can be incredibly useful. Imagine receiving a daily report that highlights the traditional and online media exposure of your company as well as that of competitors and also analyzes it for a share of voice. If members of your executive team can receive the report via e-mail clickable links that enable all team members to read relevant articles—even if they are behind a paywall, it's a powerful tool.

ONLINE CRISIS MANAGEMENT

When you're caught in a communications situation of any kind, particularly in a crisis, it is vital that an organization speaks. And there should be one voice, meaning that any official communications from the organization should come from a designated spokesperson. A clear relations policy can be invaluable as it serves as a reminder to that only authorized spokespeople should communicate with members of the press, and it also offers guidance on how to handle media inquiries.

Through web searches, review sites, antisocial media channels, the Internet has become the front door for most businesses. In most cases, the first impression and the initial perception that people have about you and your company will come through the web.

Major brands most probably will have hate sites: Apple, McDonald's, Coca-Cola, Chevy and so on, have them. The sites are accessible, but they don't appear high in search results when you're looking for general information on the brands. Companies have so much positive information on the web, and customers who author positive reviews ensure that the good news drowns out the bad. All businesses aren't as fortunate. However, at times, a few negative reviews can be killers...

SOCIAL CURRENCY

Marketers, one of the coolest things about the web is that when an idea takes off, it can propel a brand or company to fame and fortune for free. Whatever you call it—viral, buzz or word-of-mouth marketing—people telling your story drives action. Many viral phenomena are products of what was started innocently: Somebody creates a funny video clip, a cartoon or a story to friends. Then one person sends it to another, and that person sends it to a different person, and this goes on and on. The creator might have expected to reach at most a few dozen friends, but the result is something way more.

REPUTATION SCORE CALCULATOR

As a prudent business owner, you've likely taken the time and necessary measures to build your credit rating as you understand that a high credit score provides your company with certain advantages such as better terms with your suppliers and a lower cost to borrow money. Well, there is another critical score that business owners need to pay attention to and that is known as an online reputation score.

With more consumers than ever turning to the Internet to research products and services before making a purchase, your company's online reputation can either help or hurt the opportunity to earn more business. For this reason, several online reputation management tools have evolved to not only help enterprises to build their image online but also to maintain it in a favorable light.

Recover any issues that may occur. In the past, online reputation management was something that only larger companies had the budgets to accommodate. However, since it has become increasingly affordable, many small businesses are also now monitoring how the public perceives their brands on the Internet.

There are several excellent resources out there that your business can take advantage of to determine its online reputation score and learn about areas that it could improve on. Business Insider recently highlighted a few of these resources, and I recommend that you check them out to see how your own business matches up.

Klout: This score uses a scale of 1 to 100 and is primarily based off of how influential your business is on the Internet. The more influential you are and the more online reach you have, the higher your Klout score will be. For example, a public figure like President Barack Obama has a Klout score of 99, and this score was determined based off of his active Facebook and Twitter accounts (and the number of fans and followers that he has on these sites) as well as having the most important Wikipedia page online. According to Klout, the average score is 40.

PeerIndex: For many businesses, their primary goal of using social media is to define themselves as an authority figure in their industry. If this is your objective, knowing your PeerIndex online reputation score is essential. This score, too, is based on a scale of

1 to 100 and essentially measures your online authority by determining how your audience values the content that you share.

PeerREACH: This tool is unique from the other online reputation management resources. It rates your business based on the quality of followers that you have on various social media channels.

To indeed manage your online reputation, business owners should take a proactive approach and actively monitor the online discussions taking place online. Whether it's social media, review sites or blogging, being on top of the online forum can help turn negative conversations into positive customers.

All of this should reinforce the fact that now is the right time to focus on improving your Reputation Score and overall online presence.

"It takes many good deeds to build a good reputation, and only one bad one to lose it."

— Ben Franklin

When in Doubt, Pull Out!

As you have seen in the previous chapters, it's very pertinent to improve your online reputation to save your online identity. However, there are a few steps which we can always be used in protecting your identity online. We call it six simple steps. You can remember this an acronym called PLS PWC. Understanding what these specific rules are, can help you in saving your identity online, and they can also save you from a lot of mishaps.

Here are the six points of PLS PWC.

P Stands for Password

Your password should be protected at all cost. You should guard your password and should not share your password with anybody else. It should not be a simple password which includes your name, your phone number or your date of birth. The password should be strong enough so that nobody else could guess your password.

L Stands for Location

We all have a smartphone, and our smartphones have GPS technology. A lot of us keep our GPS on and don't turn it off when it's not needed. Giving away your location can be an extremely dangerous thing for you and a blessing for hackers and other people who are looking to hack your identity online. So, whenever you are traveling, whenever you don't need to give your location, turn off the GPS.

S Is from https

While making any transaction online, especially when you are looking to do some sort of financial transaction, always look for the secured site and see if it's the https website. Check if the link is there which can be seen on your address bar when you are typing a website address. Https makes it very clear that the website is secured and all your online transactions that are happening have been checked by the authorities.

P Stands for Privacy

We have already spoken about your privacy settings of social media platforms and Google and other channels. Always keep your privacy settings as private, and you can always check that all your posts are not in the public domain. You don't want them to be in the public domain. They must be seen only by your friends are your friends and family.

W Stands for Wi-Fi

Please don't look for free Wi-Fi whenever you are outside your house. You should be wary about a free Wi-Fi and should not use it often. If you don't have any other options, then only go with the secured Wi-Fi network as free Wi-Fi network is the easiest way through which hackers can get into your system or your mobile phone and can hack and can take care of your online identity.

C Stands for Click

Always think before you click on any of the websites or any of the emails as their lots of clickbait, and a lot of lots of clickbait companies which are working currently.

To finish this book, I would like to comment on the part that protecting your online privacy and protecting an identity is very difficult as there is no guarantee that your precautions will protect you. We have this only one way to hack, and hackers can try everything to do that. However, it's in our hands to protect our own online identity and protect ourselves from these threats. But in the end, the golden rule will always be: If you are in doubt, just pull out. If you are in doubt, just log out of that place. Gut feeling is the most important part which human beings have. If you think that something is wrong if you feel that there is something is fishy going on, just log out. It will save you from a lot of trouble.